SANDALS IN THE SNOW

SANDALS IN THE SNOW

A True Story of One African Family's Journey to Achieving the American Dream

DR. ROSE IHEDIGBO, CEID, CEIS

YorkshirePublishing

www.yorkshirepublishing.com

Write Now.

ISBN: 978-1-947247-49-9
Sandals in the Snow
Copyright © 2013 by Rose Ihedigbo

Scripture quotations marked (NASB) are taken from the *New American Standard Bible®*, Copyright © 1960, 1962, 1963, 1968, 1971, 1972, 1973, 1975, 1977, 1995 by The Lockman Foundation. Used by permission.

For permission requests, write to the publisher at the address below.

Yorkshire Publishing
3207 South Norwood Avenue
Tulsa, Oklahoma 74135
www.YorkshirePublishing.com
918.394.2665

DEDICATION

This book is dedicated to all who have sojourned in faith, triumphed in hardship, and committed themselves to the labor of love in serving the needy, poor, and helpless;

To College Church family, whose love, kindness, support, and generous giving have been the showcase of God's love;

To my children, Onyiyechi, Emeka, Nathaniel, David and James, who have persevered in upholding the truth passed down to them from Mom and Dad;

To the honor of the late Rev. Dr. Apollos Ndulaka Ihedigbo, whose teaching and legacy will always remain with us as in the writing of Solomon:

> My son [daughter], observe the commandments of your father,
> And do not forsake the teaching of your mother,
> Bind them continually on your heart,
> Tie them around your neck
> When you walk about, they will guide you,
> When you sleep, they will watch over you,
> And when you awake, they will talk to you.
> For the commandment is a lamp, and the teaching is light.
>
> Proverbs 6:20–23 (NAS)

You all taught me to *never* give up. To God be the *glory*!

ACKNOWLEDGEMENTS

To my children, Onyii, Emeka, Nathaniel, David and James, whose stories have brought tears to my eyes, laughter to my mouth, and joy to my spirit. You will always remain special to me. My prayers to God on your behalf and on behalf of my grand-children will always be my commitment.

My special thanks to Dr. Shannon Cormier, who labored with me to write this book, spending endless hours interviewing and gathering stories for this project.

To Dr. Daniel and Mrs. Evelyn Okorafor, for their input and guidance that helped to build the stories.

To Esther Harris, who has been my best friend for more than fifteen years.

To Patrick Smith, whose longtime friendship with the family and his devotion to the work in Nigeria sometimes make us think that he is Igbo.

To my daughter-in-law Kara, who devoted time in reading and editing the manuscript.

Thank you and may the Lord bless and reward you.

TABLE OF CONTENTS

A BRAND-NEW LIFE BEGINS

Who knew so many white people existed in the world? Rose asked herself as she and her three small children walked timidly through New York's John F. Kennedy International Airport, huddling together as they pushed through the crowds of other travelers that buzzed around them. Everyone seemed to be in such a great hurry. In her arms, she held her youngest, one-year-old Nathaniel (Nate), while three-year-old daughter, Onyii, clutched her mother's leg with one hand and her two-year-old brother Emeka's hand with her other.

The plane ride over from Nigeria was an experience unlike any they'd ever encountered; how such a huge monstrosity of a machine plane could sustain itself in the air, over the ocean no less, confounded them throughout the duration of the flight. As she'd peered out of the window at the vast expanse of water below them, all Rose could do was shake her head in wonder.

However, arrival at this hub of fast-moving, non-stop activity was an adventure of its own. This young Nigerian mother's first foray onto American soil was thrilling, terrifying, exciting, and confusing all at once. The unusual sights, the sounds, the smells—some pleasant, and some not—the people of every shape, size, and most of all, color that walked at fast paces intently through the terminal were enough to make her want to stop and take it all in, beholding this experience that overwhelmed her senses. Instead, she continued, for she was focused on a mission: to navigate this enormous, intimidating building and find her husband, Apollos, who was waiting for them somewhere in this vast monstrosity. Thus, through the airport she walked, guarding her children and her carry-on possessions carefully, for they were all she had remaining of the life she'd left behind in Nigeria to begin this new one. Eyes wide open, she carefully read and followed the directional signs: U.S. Customs, International Travelers, Main Terminal, Restaurants, Baggage Claim, Ground Transportation.

After walking for what seemed like miles, waiting in lines that seemed to move at the pace of the snails that climbed the outer walls of her home back in the village, and making her way of crowds as thick as the Nigerian bush from which she came, she finally saw him: Apollos—her husband, her lover, and her friend. The love of her life stood just directly ahead, off to the left with the biggest grin humanly possible, one so big, in fact, it could have easily registered with Guinness. She caught his eye.

"Enyi! Enyi! Enyi!" he called out loudly in his noticeable Nigerian accent as he waved wildly in her direction. He did not call her by her formal name, but she knew that he called for her; *enyi* meant "my partner" and "my dear friend" in their native tongue of Igbo. Bursting with relief on the inside, Rose smiled broadly on the outside, exhaling with an audible sigh of relief. In the midst of all this chaos, she had finally found her life partner, and the long journey that she had anxiously anticipated over the past year had at last come to an end. She was home.

"There's your dad!" she exclaimed to her small children who were still dazed from all of the confusing activity that buzzed around their two- to three-feet-high eye level. They barely heard their mother over all the footsteps and wheeled suitcases zipping by them on every side.

Rose rushed over to her waiting husband and gave him a kiss on the cheek. Apollos hurriedly leaned over to grab his wife and squeezed her tightly, allowing all of the months of loneliness, meals alone, cold nights, days without an embrace, and situations in which he'd longed for the wisdom that only a wife could give to melt away. Though he had been living in New York for the past year by himself, for the first time, he felt like he was home. In an instant, with his wife and children finally by his side, he felt more like himself than he had in a long time.

After sharing this eternal moment, Apollos reached down to hug each of his small children, embracing each one individually with a strong, fatherly hug that said, "You're home now. You're with Daddy now, and everything is going to be all right!"

After gathering their suitcases, African cloth bags, and other belongings and making ready to head for the busy airport's exit, Apollos stopped short in his tracks, suddenly realizing what was draped across his arm—a pile of coats and blankets.

"I almost forgot! Put these on!" he excitedly exclaimed to his family. "It's cold outside!" He distributed the second-hand coats that he'd meticulously picked out for his wife and children.

Rose, Onyii, Emeka, and Nate had no concept of the cold that awaited them outside of the airport terminal, but they would soon experience it the moment they stepped outside into the icy snow—in their open African sandals! This was to be the first of many unusual experiences in the place that would be their new home. The life that Rose had known and loved back in her African country of Nigeria was now a thing of the past, and her new life was ready to begin.

Onyii, Emeka, and Nathaniel sat quietly on the sofa of their uncle's house, wearing all white. Through the long colorful piece of cloth that covered the front door, shielding the indoors from the dusty elements outside, they could hear the familiar activity of their father's village buzzing, even picking up occasional snippets of conversations being held between their extended family members. Three year-old Onyii was unclear of where they were going, only that she and her two younger brothers had been carefully put together by their mother and had to sit perfectly still in order to ensure that their neatly pressed clothing did not get a wrinkle or become smudged with the red African dirt just beyond the front door.

The house in which they sat was in their paternal grandmother's compound within the village; though it was not the largest house in the compound, her father's eldest brother held this claim to the compound fame. Though he was one of the wealthiest and his house was the largest and grandest of everyone else's in the compound, it was considered to be so according to the subjectivities of locals, mostly very poor ones; Westerners laying eyes on the humble abode might opt to call it merely adequate. However, it was the house of her father's first younger brother in which Onyii and her brothers sat, patiently waiting for what lay ahead of them. His house was respectable as village houses go.

Apollos Ihedigbo's village, Umuawa, was approximately two miles long and was the home of about 1,200 people. Each village is generally organized in the same fashion, being comprised of several compounds. Within each of these compounds existed a group of people living in an interdependent world of their own.

The compound was a cluster of houses of every shape and size arranged in a not-so-exact rectangle on its own patch of lush green rural paradise. The main road at the very top of the compound marked the point through which people, most often residents and their guests from neighboring villages, entered the close-knit community. This village was a typical one, teeming with children, many barefoot, playfully chasing one another around with lots of giggles; mothers hand-washing their family's laundry in metal washtubs; fathers sitting on stools, tubs, and other makeshift seating in small groups, discussing the latest village news; and young people trying to figure out how they could make it into the city to get caught up in something more interesting and fun.

Umuawa was not unlike most other villages in Umuahia. People were born here, raised here, schooled here, courted here, married here, bore children, and started the cycle all over again with their own families. Because the village was comprised of one group of people of one blood, it was forbidden to marry within the same village.

Every family knew the other families in the village—and their business. It was hard to keep a secret in such a close-knit community of people who were of the same blood, the same background, and joined in such an intimate way at the heart. In fact, in the village, there existed a closeness among kin that few Westerners will ever enjoy, no less understand, as a result of the spirit of rugged individualism bred in them from the time of birth.

Every celebration that an individual was privileged to enjoy was not simply a family matter, but a matter of the village. In the same fashion, every tragedy that a family encountered was not one that it had to suffer through alone because the village was there to share the grief. Because of this, no one among them had need. One family would never dare stand by to see a member of the village suffer without food, shelter, clothing, or any of the other vital necessities of life if it was in their power to give. They shared everything—one heart, one mind, one soul—that was the typical village.

On the other hand, this particular compound of the village in which Onyii and her brothers sat—the compound of their paternal grandmother—was not so typical; a mere glance around the compound and anyone could easily see why. In the middle of the compound sat something of an anomaly when compared with other compounds—a grave. Right there, smack in the middle of the cluster of houses that comprised the beloved Ihedigbo compound sat the grave of Ada, the mother of Apollos and his five siblings.

Those who were new to the compound would instantly stop and pause, head cocked to the side in curious consideration at such a sight. The quizzical look that would cross their faces would be followed by the inevitable question, "That isn't a *grave*, is it?" Then the recipient of the question would be compelled to gingerly explain the meaning behind the grave that sat uncharacteristically in the middle of the Ihedigbo compound.

"You see, that is the grave of Ada Ihedigbo. She was buried in this position of honor in the center of the compound because she was a daughter of the compound, but she was…uhm…different," the reply would come with a midsentence clearing of the throat for effect.

"What do you mean, 'different'?"

"Let me put it this way: *she* was different because all of her children look different…for a reason."

This was followed by offering the inquirer an intent look with a slight sideways nod accompanied with the raise of an eyebrow as if to say, "You know what I mean?"

The story of Ada Ihedigbo made for a slightly uncommon dynamic in Umuawa and in her father's compound because Ada had borne children from six different fathers. When a woman from an Igbo village gets married, she is expected to leave her own compound to go and live in her husband's, never to return again. In the case of Apollos' mother, she did marry and moved to a different place; however, in time, she returned back to her father's compound—the one where she was born—and brought her children back to the compound with her. Only some of them, excluding Apollos, actually knew their fathers.

Needless to say, her return was greatly frowned upon. Over time, Ada's children began to prosper over and above her relatives' children that lived in the compound. As a result, her relatives felt unfortunate; after all, how else could these fatherless children be prospering more than them, the true owners of the compound?

It was for this reason that there were so many constant quarrels and misunderstandings in the compound. In fact, though Ada was allowed to be buried in the center of the compound— the only space available for a burial at the time—because she was a daughter of the compound, when her son Apollos passed away later on in life, he was buried on purchased land outside of the compound because the relatives would not allow for his burial within the compound. While the residents of the compound did permit his mother to be buried in the compound, she would be the only exception; neither Apollos nor any of his siblings would ever enjoy this privilege.

Though such was the unusually dramatic situation in Apollos's village, his wife Rose's village of Umuda was a bit more subdued—a bit more typical. This village was also very community-centered and considered itself family, most of all, because it was. Not only did many of them share the same name, they shared the same DNA in their strong, undiluted, 100 percent African blood. Most of all, they shared the same love for one another and their families.

When you hear that it takes a village to raise a child, the village of Umuda characterized the concept completely. Here, no individual or family owned a child; rather, every child belonged to the entire village. In the village, there would be no such thing as paid childcare; no one would pay for such an unnecessary expense when the youngster belonged to anyone who knew his name.

As children ran around engaging in their usual antics, it was commonplace for a member of the village—whichever adult saw a child up to no good—to immediately discipline the child on the spot without so much as a word to the child's parents. This was an accepted practice, as the parents knew that the other villagers loved their children as much as they themselves did and would never do anything to harm their little ones.

As a result of such discipline that was ready to be dispensed at any given moment, being right around the corner everywhere they went, children were much more conscious of their behavior; they always knew someone was watching. Even more, this style of discipline extended into the school; teachers could not provide an adequate education to students who are not focused on their lesson, so they disciplined the children in the classroom just as easily and then put them back to work.

Rose's village was clean, organized, and peaceful. On a certain day, everyone would come out of their homes in the different compounds and clean the village, picking up pieces of paper and plastic that might have accumulated in a common gathering spot, sweeping up dry grass, leaves, and candy wrappers from the dirt pavement in common areas in order to make it clean and clutter-free. After all, just because it was a dirt pavement did not mean it had to *look* dirty; thus, they put their small straw brooms to work, bending over to sweep and clean their village and beautify their surroundings as a community.

The village of Umuda operated not as individuals, but as a true community. They would do anything to protect, support, and celebrate with the people of their village, whom they called brothers and sisters and, in the case of someone older, aunt and uncle. They loved their own, and each one protected the other.

As most of its residents were agricultural, the people of Umuda also helped one another in their farming. Everything was done as a group, and this included both work and play. They genuinely enjoyed their closeness and the time they shared with one another at meetings, fellowships, and church, as well as at celebrations of the birth of a child, traditional marriages, and even funerals. There was much to be shared in the small village, including a love for one of their favorite daughters, Rose.

Rose Ijeoma Onyebuchi was born in Umuda in the city of Umuahia, Abia state, Nigeria. She was the third born of four children: there was her sister Mary, brother Will, then Rose Ijeoma, followed by brother Nnamdi. Though she was born in this small village, her parents lived in the state of Enugu; this is where she would be raised.

Rose's father, Nelson Onyebuchi Nwokocha, was a laundry-man and dry cleaner, a profession that went by "washerman" at the time. An entrepreneur by nature, he would journey to the quarters where many British and American expats lived and develop contracts with them to provide their laundry services. Offering this service to his clients included picking up their clothing, laundering them, ironing them, and then recruiting his children to accompany him back to the expats' quarters with the fresh, crisp washed and ironed clothes neatly packaged. Upon their delivery, the people would hand over their money along with their next batch of dirty laundry to be serviced. It was in this way that Nelson made a humble living for his family.

Rose was happy to perform her role in helping her father's business as any responsible Nigerian girl would. Each morning before school, she and her siblings would wake before the sun itself and walk no less than seven miles to deliver the clothes with their father. When they returned home, they would prepare for school.

Also entrepreneurial by nature, Rose's mother, Helen Onyebuchi, was a seamstress who designed, produced, and sold clothes in the local market. She was not the only one who sold her wares in the large, open-air market though, as she was sur-rounded by people selling different types of food, soaps, beauty butters, oils, cooking wares, and other living essentials. Without some very strategic efforts to stand out from the crowd, one could easily blend into the sea of the hundreds of other colorful vendors selling their wares to the thousands of people bustling through the market with their shopping bags.

It is for this reason that as soon as school ended each day, Rose and her siblings would make a beeline for their mother's little store in the market. While Mother industriously contin-ued to construct her fashions with her hand sewing machine, her children would take the ornate dresses, skirts, blouses and head wraps she'd made around the market to sell them to people they thought might look interested. Some days, they would return back to their mother's store having sold two or three dresses. Upon the presentation of the small handfuls of dirty and crumpled yet valuable bills to their mother, every one of them sported a huge grin.

It was in this structured, disciplined environment that Rose learned her ethic for hard work and determination. No matter how early you had to rise, rise up early to get the job done. No matter how tired you might be at the end of the school day, go the extra mile to help the family earn the money to put food on the table. Her family was a team, and every member of the team was to play a part. No matter how young, no one was exempt from hard work.

There could be no better reflection of the hard work and dedication to raising a successful family than that which Helen modeled before Rose and her siblings as children in Nigeria. In addition to being a hard worker, she was heavily involved and well respected in the community. Even though she did not receive education through formal schooling, Helen was one of the most learned of women, filled with the wisdom and knowledge that developed as a result of her voracious appetite for information about everything around her; she absorbed such knowledge from people she met and experiences that she encountered and from every opportunity presented to her in life.

When a stranger met Helen, that person was not a stranger for long. Masterful in building relationships and influencing people, Rose's mother was a grassroots organizer par excellence, working with various community organizations and even in the political realm. In fact, she had been so effective in her involvement with organizing political rallies and activities that when Queen Elizabeth made her official diplomatic visit to Nigeria, Helen Onyebuchi was right there, a part of the group that supported the Queen's visit. Rose's mother was a Nigerian legend in her own right, and over time, Rose realized how much of her mother's drive to affect change in the world passed down to her.

After Rose moved to the U.S. later in life, her mother had the privilege of visiting her daughter twice in her new country of residence. Helen thought the United States was the most beautiful thing she'd ever seen. Prior to making the journey across the waters, she believed what many other Nigerians believe about the U.S.—that it is a paradise that looks just like heaven. However, upon her arrival, as she rode in the car peering out in amazement at the massive forests, bushes, and trees, she realized that the world is the same everywhere; with its lush greenery, many places in Massachusetts resembled her own homeland of Nigeria. On the other hand, there were things like snow in Massachusetts, a very white, very cold powdery substance the likes of which she had never seen or experienced before. She quickly concluded that the cold weather was not something she'd ever want to experience again, as it chilled her to the bones.

When she returned to Nigeria after her first time visiting her daughter in the states, Helen proudly went back to her village and began to refer to herself as the American Woman; over time, so did everyone else in the village! It was a unique name, and when her fellow village members called her by this name, especially the women, she felt so proud. Few, if any others could wear such a proud label, especially from her village, because it was very uncommon for Nigerians to be able to travel to the United States. She was one of only a few that would ever have the privilege of being granted a visa and making this trip of a lifetime that other villagers would die wishing they could make.

Before she went on to be with the Lord in 2001, Helen Onyebuchi was blessed to see the great strides that her daughter and her family had made in the U.S. and how they were intent on fulfilling their covenant to give back to their native land of Nigeria. Knowing that Rose was surrounded by the loving people of the College Church, as Mother called it, and closely connected to the Nigerian network of family and friends in the U.S., she was content that her daughter was well taken care of, well loved, safe, and walking with the Lord—the most a mother could want out of life for a daughter. Most of all, Helen realized that her own passion to make an impact in the lives of others remained alive in her daughter, and about this, she was glad.

It is often said that the best relationships are like yin and yang, two different types of people that balance one another out, one offering strengths that will compensate for the other's weaknesses, tendencies, and personality flaws. The relationship of Rose's mother and father followed similar suit. While her mother Helen was very lively, outgoing, active, and influential in the community, her father was just the opposite—very laid back, very serious, and a strong, hard worker.

Nelson Onyebuchi Nwokocha was dedicated to providing for his family and being a good father. Though he loved his children in a strong, silent way, he disciplined them strongly out of this same love. Nelson was a well-known man in the village in which the family lived. Unlike his wife, Helen, however, he never had the opportunity to visit the United States before his passing in April of 1977.

The proud, feisty product of Nelson and Helen, their daughter Rose enjoyed a very happy yet serious upbringing in their home. Though the home's atmosphere could not necessarily be described as a fun one, there was a certain level of happiness that a young child could experience in a home that was as strict, serious, intense, and hardworking as hers. The work that she and her siblings contributed towards the family's businesses and the upkeep of the household was simply a part of life; rather than look down upon their before- and after-school duties, they saw it as teamwork—what it took to survive. Unlike today, when children often view the responsibility of providing for and maintaining the household as solely a parental responsibility, Rose and her siblings were happy to be regarded as significant enough to be a part of the team and shoulder some of the effort.

Rose's mother stood outside of her front door, gazing intently down the path that led into the compound. With her hands on her hips, she leaned back on the side of the house to rest from the work she'd already put in the first few hours of the day. Already, the compound was bustling with activity—mothers gathering sticks and straw, preparing fires to make breakfast, children washing themselves outdoors on the sides of the houses with water that had been warmed on the fire, men bundling up the wares that they would sell at the market for the day.

Before long, Helen saw her children coming down the path, followed by Nelson, who had just made the daily round trip with his children to deliver the fresh packages of laundry that he had washed, ironed, and packaged up the day before, working late into the night. Her small clan had been walking for fourteen miles now—seven miles each way—but now it was time for them to hurry up and prepare themselves for school. Each of the children trudged along the path with a small bag of clothing, reserving the largest and heaviest bag for their father, who was relieved to be home for the day.

"Ijeoma! Ijeoma! Hurry up! You have a big day at school today!" her mother called out as she went into the house to get breakfast on and pack lunches.

Ijeoma rushed into the house and dropped her bag in the designated corner of the house where her father sorted the laundry and ran over to the washbasin. Her mother had already heated water for her to wash her face and wipe down her dusty little feet. After washing behind her ears and neck and brushing her teeth, she proceeded to the bed where her mother had carefully laid out her green school uniform. She stood for a moment and admired it.

"Ijeoma!" her mother called out again. "What are you doing in there?"

"I'm almost ready, Mama!" Ijeoma called back. She knew that she was running a bit late today, and the three-mile walk to school would be lonely if she and her siblings had to go by themselves. Her mother was trying to ensure that they were on time to make the walk with the other kids from the compound.

At Ijeoma's school, as with all of the schools that served the towns, students wore uniforms. Though they did not have much money at all, parents that sent their children to school had to make room to afford a uniform, which they would wash every couple of days in order to keep it fresh. Rose was fortunate; her mother was a seamstress, so she had several green uniforms, and she wore these dresses proudly as she walked through out of compound and towards the school with her siblings.

School was very special for Rose because going to school was a big deal. Not all of the kids in her town went to school, and though many of them did not go because they did not desire to go, others did desire to go but did not have the resources to do so.

In the Onyebuchi household, however, school attendance was not a choice—it was a mandate. Nelson and Helen were intent on their children getting an education because they themselves did not have the privilege to do so. Even if she'd had a choice in the matter, Rose would have easily volunteered to go to school because she loved it. She equally loved reading, math, and science, being the first to jump up and volunteer when the teacher asked for volunteers to read aloud and feeling a tremendous sense of competence and confidence when she was the first to successfully solve a math or science problem. Each of these topics she studied in the one, same class with the one same teacher for one full year at the school, and each day, she grew more deeply and more passionately in love with learning and the world of opportunity that education offered her.

When it came to religion, most of the people in the village of Umuda participated in one of two types: traditional religion or Christian religion. Followers of traditional ancestral religion worshipped their gods in the village and chose to use traditional medication and libations for healing and the treatment of various physical, emotional, and mental ailments. Christians, on the other hand, worshipped the eternal God; however, there were variations in their beliefs about how He was to be worshipped.

In the African tradition, "Christian" simply means that one is not Muslim—that an individual goes to church instead of a mosque or even that someone does not go to church at all, as is the case with those who practice traditional ancestral religion. Thus, a Christian can refer to someone who is traditional and ancestral, Roman Catholic, Methodist, Presbyterian, or any range of non-Muslim denominations.

In Rose's family, her mother and father were Christians in the Nigerian sense—they wore this label because they were not Muslims. Rose's mother took her and her siblings to church every Sunday. Rose's father, on the other hand, did not participate in church, though he did allow his wife and children to attend. While he did acknowledge that there was a God in heaven, that was the extent of his Christianity.

Despite these differences in worship style, Rose's village of Umuda was paradise to her. It was here that she was born, here that she played, here that she learned the domestic duties of a wife, and here that she lived when she came to develop a very real, very intimate relationship with Christ on her own in 1970. The context under which she came to know Him, however, was one that she would not wish on her worst enemy.

DIVINE APPOINTMENTS: THE BIAFRAN WAR AND SCRIPTURE UNION DAY CAMP

More than 250 ethnic groups exist in Nigeria. While a common African blood joins them, they are often divided by traditions surrounding their political, social, tribal, and religious beliefs and practices. These differentiating characteristics led to intense interethnic rivalry, accusations of preference for one group over another, political instability, and an overall sense of anarchy mostly among the major ethnic groups: the Islamic Hausa/Fulani in the north, the Yoruba in the west, and the Christian Igbo in the southeastern part of Nigeria.

In 1960, in a well-intentioned effort to bring some unification to the division that existed among the segmented people of its nation, Nigerian leaders developed a plan to become a federation of three regions that were based on ethnic groupings. However, not all parties were happy with this new federation, namely the state of Biafra, which, in 1967, attempted to secede from the Nigerian federation.

From May 30, 1967, to January 12, 1970, the Nigerian Civil War, also known as the Biafran War or the Nigerian-Biafran War, wreaked havoc throughout the vast nation. After all was said and done, historians would estimate from one million to three million Nigerian Igbos dying in the war as a result of battle deaths, deaths by political violence, and starvation as a result of widespread famine. More than half of the deaths were civilians.

Additionally, thousands of Igbos lost their lives in the bitter three-year civil war, and an estimated two million Igbos fled to the east from various parts of Nigeria. Marked by intense fighting, genocidal practices, guerilla-war tactics, inhumane shortages of medicine, food, and housing, and shelter and a massive displacement of more than three million Igbos, the Biafran War changed the course of a generation, particularly that of Rose and Apollos Ihedigbo who found themselves right in the middle of it as youth trying to make their way in the world.

During the Nigerian-Biafran War, Rose was a young woman. In addition to their villages being bombed, local Igbos had consistently suffered harassment at the hands of the troops that infiltrated the Igbo territories in which they lived. As a result of this vicious war that waged around her village and throughout her nation, all schools had been closed for some time. Throughout those thirty months that the war continued, there was little else for school-age youngsters to do other than hang out with another, wasting much time doing nothing at all.

It was during this season of mass violence and unspeakable conflict that Billy Roberts, a white British missionary, arrived in Nigeria. His purpose: to organize Christian day camps called Scripture Union Groups for young students who needed an escape from the horrific conditions that surrounded them day to day by providing them with fun activities, lessons about Christ, and, best of all, food. He would provide them a very nice, healthy lunch each day, and this was a major attraction for young people witnessing near starvation all around them.

While she had grown up as a Christian, in the Nigerian sense of the term, she did not really know Christ personally. However, at the Scripture Union Group camp, she had an encounter with Christ that would forever change the course of her life. In April 1970, while attending Christian day camp, Christ was preached to a spiritually hungry eighteen-year old Rose Onyebuchi, and she gave her life to Christ.

As soon as the altar call was made for young people that wanted to accept Christ, she leapt out of her seat and walked forward, moved with a deeply intense, sincere passion to embrace the Savior that had died for her sins. When she finished inviting the Lord into her life, Rose didn't feel much. She knew she had been sincere, but she had expected to feel something much more deep and intense—much more affirming—than that which she felt when she rose from prayer and went back to her seat. In any case, she knew that she was saved, and she was glad about it.

As soon as Roberts began his day camp in the area, word spread among young Nigerian Christians like wildfire. "There is a white missionary here who will *feed* you *and* let you play games!" the young people would enthusiastically share with one another. When they finally ventured out to visit the camp for the first time, they were not disappointed. In addition to leading the young adults in physical activities like running, skipping, and field games, there was lots of fun in playing board games and other fun indoor activities. It was a safe, enjoyable, and loving place for young people to hang out in such a time as this. Most of all, it was a place where young people could begin and develop a relationship with Christ, learning that living in a close, real relationship with the Lord as a Christian could be quite fun.

Working at the Scripture Union Group camps to serve the more than three hundred young Nigerians from various village each day were the white family members of Roberts. There were also some Africans who had become Christians through his ministry that worked in the camp alongside them.

The format for Scripture Union Groups filled the void for school that so many young people had missed out on during and after the war, for it was operated similarly to a school itself.

When the youth arrived at nine o'clock in the morning, they would begin the day with church assembly, singing songs out of the Scripture Union booklets that each young believer had been given. It was here that Rose learned the chorus of a song that remains dear to her heart even to this day:

> Let the beauty of Jesus be seen in me
> All His wondrous compassion and purity
> O Thou Spirit Divine—all my nature refine
> 'Til the beauty of Jesus be seen in me!

After a time of singing, the missionary would preach his message. Following this, the young people were divided into different groups in which they would play games, which were followed by what was secretly everyone's favorite time of the day—lunch.

Lunchtime at Scripture Union was a very special time. Eagerly marching towards the dining hall in anticipation of what the day's nice meal would be, the students would try not to appear so eager, though sometimes they could barely contain their excitement. They were truly grateful for the delicious rice, farina, soup, sandwiches, and other goodies that they would never have at their homes back in the village. The poverty that was brought on by the war forbade it to be so.

After lunchtime, everyone would again be broken out into different groups for Bible study, prayer, and discipleship. Towards the end of the afternoon, all of the young people would gather again for a final group session and close in prayer for the day. At 3:00 p.m., Scripture Union was over, and everyone made his or her trek back to the village, only to rest and return to the camp the next day.

After being saved, Rose instantly knew that she was called to walk with God in a great way, but this would require learning how to lead. However, it did not take long for Rose to begin to develop as a leader in the things of God as a result of the things she'd learned and experienced at the Scripture Union camp. As a result, not long after she'd given her life to Christ, Rose was placed over a Scripture Union Group chapter that was started in her own village; though it only met on Sundays, it quickly became one of the best the organization had. It was while serving as the leader of this local group that Rose realized it was her heart's passion to help other young people get to know Christ. However, she could not help but to vividly recall the *first* time she was called to lead out in prayer in the group.

During the time immediately following the end of the war, which had just ended less than two years prior, there were still no schools, no food, and no productive activities for young people. Everything remained closed, having either been destroyed by the war, cut off from suppliers who blockaded the import of resources into the area during the war, or having their owners either killed, maimed, or threatened to such an extent that they were unwilling to reopen so soon after the terrible conflict.

Each day thereafter, a group of young people walked from Rose's village to go to day camp, braving whatever elements they encountered along the dirt road to reach their destination. Whatever it took, including making a ten-mile walk, they were determined to attend the day camp every one of the five days a week that it was open.

On this particular day, the young believers sat in a small circle under the tent that housed the day camp. Around them sat other young adults in small clustered circles of their own, speaking in softer-than-usual voices so as not to disturb the other groups around them. These small groups were prayer groups, designed to mentor the young believers in how to pray, and in them, each person in the group was called upon to pray in his or her own way.

Though Rose had prayed before, she had never prayed like *this*; she didn't know what to say or do as she sat there wringing her hands with her eyes closed, so nervous that she barely heard the petitions towards God that her other group members were speaking. Beads of sweat rolled down the sides of her face and back, not because of the heat she felt sitting under the large tent, but because of the uneasy anxiety she felt at the prospect of praying before others this day.

With each new voice she heard beginning a new prayer, she would inconspicuously open one eye in that direction, noticing that each time, her turn to pray was inching closer and closer, person by person. They prayed sincerely and passionately in the circle, and as one person prayed, the others called out their agreement with the words being spoken.

"Yes, Lord!" they would say. "Do it God!" they would earnestly plead aloud.

Finally, as the young lady beside her began to wind down in her prayer, Rose braced herself. Holding her breath for a few seconds to slow down her near hyperventilation, she closed her eyes tightly, balled her fists, opened her mouth, and began to pray.

Rose didn't know what had happened to her. She prayed with the strongest, boldest, most confident spirit she could muster up, forgetting where she was sitting, who was around her, and even forgetting herself. As she prayed, she was caught up in the way that people often see themselves caught up in a dream, almost as if she was not there speaking at all. This was mostly true because this day, the Spirit took over the young woman's mouth, and instead of praying out of her mind and intellect, she prayed out of her belly, allowing rivers of living water to gush from the deepest depths of her being. When she finished, the prayer passed on to the next person, but Rose sat in her chair enraptured with what she had just experienced. It was the most intense feeling she'd ever felt.

What had happened to her, she did not know. For the life of her, she would never be able to adequately explain it again. All she knew was that from the time of closing the prayer, even as she left the meeting and walked the ten miles along the dirt road back to her home in the village, she felt like something very special had happened in her heart. She knew that she had truly accepted the Lord in a very real, intimate way and that something quite beautiful and awesome had just happened to her. Even as she prayed, she gave her entire life to the Lord, including her goals, her dreams, her agenda, and her ambitions, and she took on His yoke, which would compel her to live her life for Christ in service to others from this day on. As she walked along the road reflecting on these things, Rose wore a permanent smile that not even the bleak conditions around her could wipe away.

THE PLAN, THE PROPOSAL, AND THE COVENANT

Rose had always enjoyed a fondness for Apollos Ihedigbo. While their home villages were very similar and a very close walking distance—less than three miles away—to one another (in fact, they shared some of the same village boundaries), they did not actually meet until they both attended the same Scripture Union Christian day camp immediately following the Biafran War.

Unlike Rose, Apollos was the second eldest child raised by a single parent and grew up not knowing his father. As a result, his older brother, Dibia, became the dominant male leader of the house, helping to raise him along with his sister and four brothers. Though he may have felt it, Apollos never expressed disappointment at not knowing his father. To him, if this was his life, not knowing his father must have been God's will; thus, he accepted it and moved on, working out his own goals and aspirations to achieve something greater in life.

Ada Ihedigbo, Apollos' mother, was a very hard worker that did whatever was necessary to support her family, selling all sorts of items in the market like fish and other food items to scrape out a living and put food on the table. With the assistance of his brother Dibia, Apollos's mother ensured that her children were well fed, cared for, educated, and loved.

By the time Rose met Apollos, he was a promising schoolteacher. He had attended a teacher training college and been trained to work as a teacher by the time the Biafran War broke out, but once the schools closed, he found himself in the same situation as the other young people—nothing productive to do on a daily basis, especially in a war-torn environment in which Igbos were constantly harassed. Thus, Apollos attended the Christian day camp just for the activities. Similar to Rose and hundreds of other Igbos who attended Billy Roberts's Scripture Union, Apollos gave his life to Christ in this day camp, and like Rose, he eventually became a leader in the camp, bringing a Scripture Union Sunday study group to his village that he led and organized.

When there is a genuine love that exists between Christian brothers and sisters that evolves over time into a courtship, it is often difficult to pinpoint the "special days" that many romantics record and celebrate as significant. For example, neither Rose nor Apollos would be able to tell an interested inquirer the day they actually met or the day they became more than friends. All they knew was that they loved the Lord and that His ministry was their primary focus in life. They called each other brother and sister, and in doing so, loved each other as such in the purest, most wholesome, and authentic sense possible. They shared a very close relationship in the Lord before they ever began to see each other as potential partners, walking to Scripture Union group meetings and attending various fellowships together. Rain or shine, Apollos would come to Rose's village, and together with the rest of the young adults, they would press their way to Scripture Union—even if not for more than the fact that they knew they would receive a good meal here every time.

Apollos had been on fire for the Lord for sometime before he entered the Igbaja seminary managed by Evangelical Churches of West Africa. As he delved into his studies here, he sensed that the Lord had attached great purpose to his life, and he was called to do great things. In fact, it was here that he became convinced about going to the United States to continue his studies.

Had she not left with her parents to go back to Enugu state, perhaps he would have sat down to run this idea by his dear friend Rose when it first arose in his spirit; however, her family, along with thousands of others, had only moved away to the city of Umuahia, the capital of Abia State in southern Nigeria, to escape the violence of the war. After a relative amount of peace was restored to the region, they had moved back to Enugu state, so she was no longer around.

Nonetheless, the very close friendship as brother and sister in Christ that they developed while serving and ministering together at Scripture Union camp near the village remained, and he wrote to her in Enugu state whenever he had opportunity. Rose enjoyed receiving these letters from her brother in Christ in which he spoke about what the Lord was doing in his life and how he was growing and developing his theological mind at the seminary. She loved the fact that they shared the same commitment and love for ministry with each other in a relationship that was so truly genuine.

In the fall of 1973, Apollos made plans to travel to Enugu state, taking advantage of his holiday break from seminary to enjoy Christmas with his brother Smart who lived there. Of course, knowing that his dear friend Rose also lived in Enugu state played a major role in the choosing of this particular holiday destination, as he had not seen her for more than a year and desired to communicate with her face-to-face rather than simply through the letters he sent to her through the post. However, more than going to Enugu to share in the glad holiday tidings, Apollos was going with a plan that began with a strategic letter written to his brother.

He was always cheerful this time of year, and the fact the war fighting had ended, peace had been restored in his village, and things had just about gotten back to normal gave him every reason to wear his holiday cheer on his sleeve. As he sat at his desk, he thoughtfully considered the words that he would write. Before long, he knew just what to say.

"Dear Smart, I pray that all is going well with you. Everything is well with me, and the Lord is doing great things here. I will tell you all about seminary when I come to visit you over the Christmas holiday. I am excited that I will be able to see you and our family and friends during my break. Please do me the favor of inviting Rose Onyebuchi over to your house while I am there so that I may also visit with my precious sister in the Lord. I desire to see her greatly."

As Apollos went on to finish his letter detailing his arrival and departure dates and which day Smart was to invite Rose to visit, he grew excited. He could not wait for the holidays!

Rose sat in the house of Apollos's brother Smart with her legs crossed at the ankles, her hands crossed atop her lap, and her mouth in a broad smile. She had just arrived at the house and been greeted by her friend whom she'd not seen in what seemed like forever, and she was so glad to see him; he looked well. After exchanging close hugs and excited greetings, Rose and Apollos were both reminded of how good it felt to be in one another's presence, a feeling they had not felt since Rose and her family had moved back to Enugu state more than a year ago.

As she was offered a seat in Smart's comfortable living room, she allowed her eyes to survey the room, quickly deciding that it was a relatively nice and traditional place, with the conventional sofa along the wall, side chairs, and a coffee table at the center of the room. Rose chose a seat on the sofa while Apollos sat on a chair on the other side of the room, facing her. She gazed upon the face of her friend, noticing every detail, particularly that he looked exactly the same today as he did when she'd said her final sad good-byes to him last year in Umuahia.

After the exchange of more pleasantries and sharing a few details about his trip from home to Enugu, Apollos took a long pause and a deep breath, marking the moment he would seize his opportunity.

"Rose," he carefully began, "I've been thinking about something, okay?"

As Rose listened to her friend, she realized that he'd turned a bit serious, and she was curious as to what was coming. When Apollos had his brother contact her with the invitation to come, receiving it did not come across as a surprise or shock; that he'd wanted to see her while he was in Enugu was quite reasonable, considering the fact that they had been very close friends before that time. However, that's all they were—just friends.

"Here is what I'm thinking," Apollos continued, trying to read his friend's face. "I'd like for you to pray about becoming my wife. I know that you are my sister in Christ and that you love the Lord, and I think we would be good together as husband and wife. Would you like to consider that? Will you pray to see if God will put it in your heart to be my wife?" he asked.

Rose sat silently not knowing what to say or how to begin to reply. She had never thought of Apollos as her husband before that very moment, so this was indeed a surprise.

"You don't have to give me an answer today," Apollos continued, filling the palpable silence. "Pray about it and give me an answer the next time I come back. Okay?"

Rose nodded in agreement. "Okay." She finally mustered enough voice to answer. "Yes. Let me go pray about it. I'm not sure it's going to happen, but I will at least go and pray."

Apollos was satisfied with his friend's answer. He knew that as long as Rose would pray, the Lord would move.

The rest of this historic visit between Apollos and Rose would be all a blur to her.

"Was that a discussion or a proposal?" she asked herself as she rode in the taxi back to her family's home, staring out the window in a daze. She had not told her parents anything about where she was going when she went to visit Apollos at his brother's house, as such a visit might be misconstrued or looked down upon for a single young lady and she would surely be chastised.

When she returned home, she continued to closely guard her secret; there was no need of getting her parents all excited about something she was not so sure was going to happen anyway. This was a secret between her, Apollos, and his brother and would be discussed with no one. However, keeping her promise to Apollos, she prayed to God sincerely to see what He would say.

The concept of marriage of a young woman to a young man is a fixture in traditional Igbo culture. After a young woman graduates from school, the natural progression of things in the eyes of her parents is that she will marry a good Christian man, preferably someone close to her village, and begin a family of her own. Despite this cultural expectation, at the time that Apollos lay his quasi proposal on the table before Rose to consider, she was neither looking for nor considering marrying anyone from her village. In fact, when she did take a moment to consider her prospects for marriage, she considered only that he need be a dedicated man in the service of God, a man of God that was not necessarily a minister or a pastor, but one who was as committed to the things of God as she was.

As Rose continued to pray and guard her secret closely, there were many things to be considered—things which she pondered each and every day. One thing about which Rose often wondered was why her? Why did Apollos pick her? Yes, she was considered one of the most fashionable and pretty girls around, and she was fun and outspoken, but was that what he saw? Upon deeper consideration, she decided that it was something more that Apollos had to have liked about her in order to ask for her hand as his life partner; she concluded that it was the love of Christ in her and the dedication she had given to work in Christ that inspired him to make his request.

While this was one point to be considered, there was also another worthy of deliberation: another brother in Christ who was showing interest in Rose and who lived around her locally while Apollos was away at seminary. Initially, in Rose's mind, it appeared that Apollos did not stand a chance; her interests were set on the local young man who pursued her, and he was close enough to pursue her more intently than Apollos could.

However, honoring her word, Rose continued to pray, and with every day that she prayed, the Lord knitted her heart closer and closer to the one that would eventually become her husband. It was not long before she realized that Apollos was the right man and that God had led him to her. She loved that he was kind, loving, sweet, and humble—a very good man. Above all, he was dedicated to the things of God, and they had walked together and ministered together as friends before things ever progressed to this level. Through prayer, the Holy Spirit confirmed for Rose that her answer to Apollos would be simple. Yes.

It would be another year or two after Apollos had earnestly asked for Rose's prayer and consideration before they actually agreed to be together as husband and wife. Throughout this time, he had been praying that the Lord would speak, and his faithful God rewarded his persistence in prayer with an adoring wife-to-be that loved the Lord as much as he did.

Throughout their courtship, Apollos and Rose lived in separate states. Rose remained with her family, and Apollos remained in Igbaja where he continued his studies in the seminary; thus, theirs was not the flowery, elaborate, made-for-the-movies type of love story. Instead, their courting rituals remained as simple as the humble lives they lived miles apart: they would exchange letters in the mail designed to encourage one another in Christ. Occasionally, once or twice during the year, Apollos would come to visit Rose, and the times they shared together were priceless; they would discuss the details of their lives, confess their love for one another and commitment to ministry, and meet in his village to attend church services together. The entirety of their life's focus was that of Christian mission and Christian duty.

Apollos and Rose Ihedigbo united themselves in holy matrimony on August 23, 1975, in the chapel of Queen Elizabeth Hospital in Umuahia, Abia State. It was the most beautiful wedding Rose had ever seen. Shortly afterward, as husband and wife, the Ihedigbo newlyweds traveled to northern Nigeria, where Apollos was now employed as a teacher for the Malumfashi Girls Secondary School. Their eldest daughter, Onyii, was born here in 1976. That same year, Apollos was called back to Enugu state in Igboland for the honor of participating in the official board of translators for the Living Bible into Igbo, so it was here he traveled with his wife and daughter in tow. It was here in Enugu that Emeka and Nathaniel would soon be born.

Together, in their small three-bedroom condominium, the Ihedigbos lived a simple life. While Rose worked as an elementary school teacher instructing six- and seven-year-olds, a babysitter cared for her three small children at home. Additional help came in the form of two relatives that shared the condo with the family, providing assistance with cooking, chores, and anything else that Rose needed, while other Christian brothers and sisters often stopped in to lend a hand. These extra hands were especially needful and appreciated after Apollos would later travel ahead of Rose and the children to the states, a fact to which any working mother of several small children can attest.

❦

As all great men are, Apollos has always been a planner by nature. While still enrolled as a student at the Evangelical Churches of West Africa seminary, anticipating his graduation in 1972, Apollos began to investigate the future of his education. While he would have loved to continue his graduate education in Nigeria, there was a problem: the Nigerian Department of Education did not honor his seminary degree as a bachelor's degree. Even though the seminary program was a four-year degree, the department would not give the degree any higher recognition than an associate's degree. That was only one of his challenges; there would be more.

Nigeria's then-minister of education did not recognize theological seminary degrees as liberal arts degrees. Again, though the program was a four-year degree with all the necessary coursework, seminary-degree graduates were not given equal recognition with other teachers who had graduated from traditional Nigerian universities. Thus, Apollos was faced with the prospect of completing his four-year degree being awarded non-liberal arts associate's degree status and would be unable to move to the graduate level of education, which required at least a bachelor's degree.

Not to be outdone, the tenacious young man went on a quest to find answers. Where there is a will, there is a way, he thought. Upon making various inquiries of his seminary professors about how he might overcome these obstacles, two primary prospects were placed before him. The first was to simply enroll in the Liberal Arts University in Nigeria; however, doing so would cost a lot of money, and admission was unlikely as a result of the high levels of bribery and corruption that controlled student admissions. The other option seemed more favorable to Apollos: go to the United States and study.

The idea of moving to the United States was both a thrilling and intimidating one at the same time. As was his custom, he sought the insights and opinions of his betrothed Rose concerning the matter before he allowed himself to arrive at any hard, fast conclusions, always broaching the discussions with, "Rose, here is what I'm thinking about..." Knowing the weight her opinions and feedback carried with this man of God, she considered her words carefully and spiritually, providing him with wise and thought-provoking things to consider.

It was during this crucial moment of his life that Apollos prayed to God, making a covenant that he worked to fulfill almost everyday of his life thereafter: if the Lord will allow him to leave Nigeria and get his degree in the United States, he would return to Nigeria and use his education to build his people. That was his promise.

Working through American missionaries that were teaching at the seminary in Nigeria, the Lord helped Apollos to secure admission to Houghton College, a Christian liberal arts college in New York, New York. Apollos finished his seminary education in 1975. He taught as a Bible teacher in secondary schools (comparable to American high schools) until 1976. Soon after, in 1977, Apollos worked on the team for a translation of the Living Bible. Then in 1979, Apollos, having sold his car for $200 so that he would have enough cash to survive temporarily, departed Nigeria by himself to study at Houghton College in the United States. One year later, in 1980, Rose and her three small children boarded a plane to join him.

When someone receives the opportunity to leave Nigeria and live in the U.S., it is quite a big deal. If he is a part of a church, the church will have a special send-off for him, complete with a special prayer over him by the pastors and leaders and lots of hugs, tears, well-wishing and even a love offering or two inconspicuously pressed into the palm of the hand.

The village from which the person hails is also not to be outdone or left out of the well-wishing. Customarily, the families within the village host a huge going-away party for the fortunate soon-to-be Nigerian expat, complete with music, dancing, a feast of various types of foods reserved for celebrations such as these, hugs, tears, and most of all, loads of unsolicited advice about how to safely navigate the world "out there" that was vastly different from the slow, simple, and communal village life they all enjoyed.

Like the rest of the world, most Nigerians develop a mental perception of places that they have never been through the media. As biased, fictitious, and overblown as the media is, for some reason, people tend to give it the benefit of the doubt, as it tells its own stories in its own way with whatever slant will benefit its financial backers the most. It is from this same source of media that Nigerians derive their sense of what American life will be like, and no group stands more horrified at what they perceive American life has to offer than the Christians.

"When you get to America, please do not backslide! There are many things there that will try to pull you away from the Lord and keep you from being a true Christian, so please be careful!" one would say.

"You know, they are very wild and free-living there in America. There is lots of sex, drugs, alcohol, and other things there that can cause even a strong, dedicated Christian like you to be led astray, so whatever you do, hold to God's hand and do not backslide! Do not mess up your life!" another would chime in.

"Wherever you go, take someone with you and watch your back! There are lots of guns in America, and there is shooting everywhere there because of much crime!" yet another would offer.

Christians possessed a general fear that if one of their own brothers and sisters went to America, regardless of how strong they were, if they did not backslide with all that this rich nation had to offer, they would be killed because of the guns and crime. Either way, seeing one of their own off to such a dangerous place so far from home was scary.

There was no customary going-away party for Rose and her babies as they made their final arrangements to say good-bye to their homeland and board the plane for New York State. The plan had jolted into action so quickly with applying for passports, waiting for what seemed like forever for their approval and delivery, saying good-byes, and settling all personal business, all while trying to coordinate the nearly twenty-hour flight with a mother and her three babies to fly overseas on a huge, intimidating plane that would take them to a vast, intimidating land. This process in and of itself was exhausting! By the time they received their passports, it was time to travel, and it was all they could do to hurriedly pack up all of the most precious personal artifacts they owned and make it to the airport on time.

Instead, a small group of friends and family accompanied Rose and her children to the airport, and this was as special a celebration as any for the young twenty-eight-year old who was preparing to start life anew in a foreign land. Her husband had left one year earlier in 1979, and she missed him dearly. As she rode along in the taxi with everything dearest to her (she'd caught a taxi because it was easier this way), she looked out of the window at the Nigerian landscape that passed her by, taking in the sight of every building, every tree, and every village like it would be her last time ever seeing them. She was going to miss home.

Rose realized that she was also going to miss her career. She had attended a teacher-training college to be trained as a teacher, and after completing the two-year college program, she had gotten a job as an elementary school teacher, providing instruction in reading, math, and science. She loved working with the children in the classroom and had been doing so all the way up to this time. Missing her students already, as she rode towards her destination, she prayed for their success.

Arriving at the airport, Rose unpacked the car and doled out final hugs to the close circle of family and friends who surrounded her and who loved her most. The sentiments were bittersweet. They were joyful that she had been presented with such a great opportunity as to live in America.

"When you get to America, open your eyes. Get the best out of that place and bring it back to us!" they said. "Do not come back as you left. Come back full and bring all that you have gained back to your people!"

Then as she gathered up her things, their hearts broke at the thought of life without her. Through tears, they encouraged her.

"Be careful, Sister Rose! We will be praying for God's protection over you and your family. Please be careful with the children! Don't forget to write!" they called out as teary-eyed Rose walked with her children through the departure gate. They may have said more, but Rose did not hear them, having walked out of earshot. No longer focused on what was behind her, she now walked intently ahead, focused only on the destiny that awaited her in America.

A SMALL BITE OF THE
BIG APPLE—A FRESH START
A THOUGHT ON COLLEGE

When Apollos Ihedigbo arrived in southwestern part of New York State to attend Houghton College in Genesee Valley—a Christian liberal arts and sciences college founded in 1883 and associated with the Wesleyan Church—it was bittersweet. He had finally realized his dream of traveling to and studying in the United States, but it was without his family, most of all his beloved confidante and dearest friend, Rose.

Alone and desperately lonely for his best friend, Apollos made his way at this college the best he could, making good use of the time to focus his attention on attending classes, spending hours studying, and getting to know other members of the close-knit Houghton community. One day in the future, after he'd gotten settled and established a place for his wife and small children to live in the city, he would send for them to travel over the seas to be reunited with him so that they could be a family once more.

That day came on a brisk, cold day in the winter of 1980, when Apollos and one of his Houghton friends who had a car drove to John F. Kennedy International Airport to pick up his wife and children. He knew that they would have no concept of the snow and the icy, biting wind that awaited them, so he brought along with him coats for each of them, donated by other students of Houghton. It was quite a sight to witness his wife seeing snow on the ground for the very first time. In Nigeria, the closest one would come to seeing snow was on the pages of a picture book, but there it was; it was quite a shock.

"When I saw Apollos at the airport," Rose recalls, "I remember thinking that he looked so healthy after not seeing him for a year. We were so happy to see each other, and after he greeted all of us, he had to show us how to put on hats, gloves, mittens, and even blankets because it was so cold outside. We came to New York in the wintertime with warm weather clothes and shoes. The very first lesson I learned on American soil: you don't wear sandals in the snow! Fortunately, we did not have to walk too long of a distance to get to where the car was. Apollos was happy, and we were so happy to be reunited as a family at the time that even though the cold was incredibly uncomfortable, we barely paid attention to it. We were finally together again. We were home."

In the car, on the drive to the small off-campus apartment where Apollos was living at the time, they chatted away happily, taking in every one of the unusual sights of the new place that would serve as the backdrop for this new phase of life at Houghton College.

The small, close-knit Wesleyan community at Houghton College was a close and loving one, taking Apollos in as their brother as soon as he'd arrived. Understanding how difficult it must be for him to come to a new country and start a brand-new life with very little, they also took his family under their wings, providing them with clothing and money to cover their necessities and assisting them in any other way they could.

One elderly New York couple in particular had taken a special liking to Apollos, adopting this international student as their own even before his family flew down to reunite with him. Mr. and Mrs. Beckwith, a pair of loving and benevolent senior citizens, were a godsend. Once Apollos's small family arrived, the couple adopted the entire family, bringing them food, driving them to the grocery store whenever necessary, taking the children to Sunday school, and offering them support in any way possible.

While Apollos and Rose took classes at Houghton, Mr. and Mrs. Beckwith would even pick up the children and take them to their home, supplying them with all of the hot chocolate and Mrs. Beckwith's fresh-baked chocolate chip cookies they could eat, followed by playtime in the couple's big backyard. Such support made life easier for the Ihedigbos to complete their classes with a sense of peace; they were good people who loved their children and who would care for them as their own. The Beckwiths served as the Ihedigbos' adoptive parents for the two years that they lived in New York, and Rose and Apollos thanked God for them daily.

The Ihedigbos also enjoyed fellowship with Nigerian brothers and sisters like Amos and Charity Nwokonna, a Nigerian couple that lived at Houghton College during the same time as the Ihedigbos. For Apollos and his young family, being able to fellowship with another family that was not only Nigerian but also shared knowledge of their same, familiar surroundings back home made this large new world a little smaller and not so intimidating. Together, they shared meals and stories of their homeland as well as study notes and stories about school, for they all took classes at Houghton together.

In their very first American apartment, Rose tried to maintain at least a small sense of the traditions of her homeland. Nowhere could she do this more successfully than in her kitchen by making her traditional Nigerian recipes. Especially on special occasions, like when these close and dear Nigerian friends came over, Rose would recruit Charity for kitchen duty, and together they would make *fufu* (a thick dough-like African food usually made out of pounded yam and used to scoop up stews and soups) and *eba* (a firm dough made from cassava flour) for the men. The making of stockfish and *eba*, a traditional Nigerian dish that consisted of a level of preparation much too cumbersome for daughter Onyii's liking, consisted of using a saw to cut up the stockfish, boiling it until it got soft, and then using the boiled stockfish to make a stew; however, the smell of the stockfish was not for the faint of heart.

The torturous smell of these Nigerian dishes was the primary reason that the Ihedigbo children often rejected traditional Nigerian food in favor of plain, old American spaghetti, while Apollos and Rose ate things like fufu, Joloff rice, and stew every day.

Not only were the children making their own adjustments to living in the U.S. early on, but Rose had to undergo her own process of adjustment. In order to get a taste of American education and culture, in September, she decided to take a class of her own at Houghton College where her husband was enrolled. One day, as they strolled down the hallways with one of their mentors, they decided to stop by the dining room to grab a bite to eat for lunch. They each took a cafeteria tray from the stack at the start of the line and walked up to the menu board. Almost instantly, Apollos and Rose exchanged puzzled looks with one another.

"What's the matter?" the mentor asked, seeing the looks they exchanged. "Do you need some help with the menu?"

"I'm not hungry. I'm not eating anything," Rose quickly quipped.

"Well..." Apollos began hesitantly, "it says 'hot dog' on the menu." He explained, "Where we are from, we do not eat dogs, and we think it very odd that Americans would eat dogs too!"

"That's right," Rose chimed in, "We absolutely do not eat any dogs. No dog meat!"

"Oh, no!" The mentor laughed heartily, hardly able to speak through his laughter. "That's just the name of the food! A hot dog is not a dog, and it is not dog meat! It is just what we call the name of the sandwich!" He went on to explain exactly what this "hot dog" was to Apollos and Rose's satisfaction. He would surely have to tuck this story into his pocket and share it with others in the future, as it was one of the funniest events he'd ever encountered with his international students!

After hearing the mentor's explanation, Rose was satisfied. She made a mental note of the second lesson she learned on American soil: hot dog is not dog meat. There was yet a lot of learning left to do in this new land!

In addition to providing a crash course in American food, Houghton also exposed young Rose to something else quite American: sports. One of the courses Rose elected to take in the fall of 1980 was tennis and volleyball, both of which she played and enjoyed greatly; however, she developed a unique fondness for tennis and even found herself particularly good at it. Even today, years later, Rose continues to play the game as a recreational activity.

"When I took my tennis and volleyball class, I found that I had a greater interest in tennis," she recollected. "Interestingly enough, when I was taking these two courses, I did not know that I was pregnant with my fourth child, David, in fact, I was in my second month or so. After playing lots of these sports several times a week, I found myself not feeling quite well. I thought it was because I had been playing so aggressively, but just to be sure, I went to the doctor for a checkup. It was there that I was surprised to learn that I was pregnant! I praised the Lord that my little son David had remained safe and God protected him from being miscarried! I took it easy after that, but I still completed the course on time and got my credits," Rose explained.

Before long, the college provided Apollos and his family with a small, cozy house in an off-campus area reserved for international students—rent-free! Not far from the Houghton community, the house was an upper- and lower-level two-bedroom apartment—both the bedrooms were upstairs and the kitchen and living were downstairs. It was a small cottage, but the Ihedigbos thought it was wonderful, even as they walked through and surveyed their new accommodations with sheer delight. The place was already furnished by Houghton who had designed it to be so, understanding that their international students came into the country with nothing.

Entering one of her favorite rooms, the kitchen, Rose took note that there were already pots and pans in the cabinets and the pantries were even stocked with food.

"Apollos, come and look at *this*!" she exclaimed holding the pantry doors wide open with both hands as she let her eyes roam up and down the boxes, bags, and cans of vegetables, soups, teas, rice, and spaghetti that she would soon begin preparing for her family's meal time. "Praise the Lord! This is *wonderful*." Rose cried out as her husband peered with pleasure over his wife's shoulder at the pantry's contents. He was grateful to God for leading him and his family to this loving Christian community who would care for them and who did not stop caring for them until they left.

The cozy little house in the city of Houghton was filled with a sense of home as well as with Rose's art that her oldest daughter Onyii clearly remembers. In fact, Rose's artwork registered so significantly with her daughter that it is the first childhood memory she has of living in the United States.

"There were drawings and paintings in the living room area against the walls," explained Onyii. "They were never really hung up, but they were pushed off to the sides in the living room. I specifically remember that they were my mom's art, and I thought she was an artist. As a four-year-old, this really impressed me and made a lasting impact on me till this very day."

When she entered Houghton College, Rose was sure that one of her majors would be art because she possessed a passionate interest in drawing. In Nigeria, she had often drawn for recreation, picking up a pencil and easily drawing it freehand in both pencil and charcoal. By the time she arrived in New York, she ventured out and began doing watercolor paintings in her spare time, even hanging some of them throughout their small cottage for decoration, adding to its warmth and vibrancy. The small children loved to sit and watch their mother create her works of art, always amazed by her ability to pick up a picture of anything and recreate it in a matter of minutes on her art pad. In their minds, here at Houghton, their young minds registered a fact: Mom is a super talented, creative genius!

Unfortunately, in the process of moving from one place to another, and in the midst of a busy life raising children and attending school, all of Rose's beautiful drawings and paintings were lost over time, and while she was an exceptional artists, she opted to study something more practical in school—childhood growth and development.

Noting their mother's creative aptitude, the Ihedigbo children searched for these same talents to be replicated in their father, but this was to no avail; Daddy couldn't draw. He did have another creative talent, however, as Rose explains.

"Apollos was creative, but he was a creative writer. His handwriting was super-duper beautiful. He wrote with excellent penmanship with the most excellent and constructive grammar, and in his free time, that's all he would do—write. Most of it was scriptural notations and Bible verses related to sermons that he was preparing from school, but he was exceptionally talented at it!"

The typical first-time New Yorker riding through the city would see many things that would arouse anyone's curiosity and cause him to instantly make the following pledge: "As soon as I get to where I'm going and get settled, I've *got* to come back out to see this, go there, eat this, explore that, and take it all in!" Such was not the case with the Ihedigbos. During their entire two years in New York, they would not see a movie, take in a show, visit a tourist attraction, or even go sightseeing through the city. Their small Houghton community was their world, and with this, they were quite content. This new environment in and of itself was a big wow experience for them, and it generated enough excitement daily to keep them planted right where they were.

Apollos and Rose's focus was not on fun, entertainment, and exposure; rather, it was on going to school and keeping their children safe—not to mention, they had neither the money nor the transportation to do anything else. In their spare time, this young family enjoyed simple recreation, taking their children for a walk through the college campus to expose them to college life or going for a walk over to the beautiful college chapel or the community Baptist church. The facilities were beautifully built with nice pews, which were neatly organized unlike anything they'd seen before. For them, *this* was entertainment and exposure.

Life was a blessing for Apollos and Rose Ihedigbo at Houghton College. Between the Beckwiths and the Walkers who provided support, babysitting services, and fellowship and the Houghton family, which generously embraced international students, they had a support system that was second to none. Apollos continued to take classes during the day while Rose scheduled her classes in the evening, when possible, to ensure that someone was always available for the children.

Houghton's care, concern, and friendliness also spilled over into the classroom. Rose explained, "We were not intimidated in the classroom. It was a mixed culture with other international students from all over Africa, including Kenya, Uganda, and other places. Our white brothers and sisters were very welcoming to us all, and the professors were Christians, so they really supported us as well. There was no room for intimidation, and this made us feel so comfortable."

Though not an intimidating one, the classrooms of Houghton College presented their own challenges for Apollos and his young wife. Though they had been trained in British phonics, their thick accents mixed with British intonations often made their words unintelligible to their American counterparts. Through close intentionality, they learned to adjust their accents when speaking and even their phonetics when writing, for example, learning to write "honor" instead of "honour." Rather than resign themselves to simply being different, they worked carefully to ensure that they did not put themselves at any disadvantage, instead opting to do whatever was necessary to be understood by their professors and fellow students. They learned to adjust in this setting, the first of many adjustments they would make in order to guarantee their success in America.

Different as they were, the international students expected the curiosity of their American classmates, many of whom had never encountered Africans in such close proximity before.

"How did you come to America?" they would ask. "Did you swim through the water?" they would inquire, blatantly displaying their innocent ignorance. "How did you learn my language?" they would ask.

It was undoubtedly clear to Apollos and Rose that many of the students here had not been exposed to Africa. In fact, many of the students they'd encountered thought that Africa was one city, while others thought that all Africans were from the same place in Africa and spoke the same languages, none of which could possibly be English. While they knew they had a learning curve as new internationals to America, Rose and Apollos knew that those Americans would have a learning curve of their own.

Apollos completed his studies at Houghton College in only two years, graduating in 1981 with a bachelor's degree. Because he had transferred to the college from the Igbaja Bible College Seminary in Nigeria, many of his classes transferred along with him, reducing the amount of time it would take him to finish the degree. Also by this time, Rose had completed five courses from Houghton with a focus on early-childhood development.

Prior to graduation, Apollos was already planning his next step: graduate school. Though his original plan had been to complete his studies at Houghton and then return with his family to Nigeria, he applied to the University of Massachusetts for a master's degree and was accepted. Thus, the family would soon be on the move again. Indeed, it would be a sad move—the detachment from such a loving Christian community that genuinely cared for them like family brought them to tears. However, in the same instant, it was a happy move—they were beginning the next phase of the life they'd dreamed of on their journey to success!

THE NEXT STEP ON THE SUCCESS JOURNEY: LIFE AT THE UNIVERSITY OF MASSACHUSETTS

After leaving Houghton College, the Ihedigbo family was Massachusetts bound. With a family that seemed to be ever growing, Apollos and Rose moved to South Deerfield, Massachusetts, choosing an older, classic '70s style home with a huge yard for their four small children as the place they would settle for this next phase in their life.

Transitioning to any place with a family is a challenge, no matter what the circumstance, and anything that can make the transition a bit smoother is welcomed with open arms. The Lord put such help in place as the Ihedigbos moved to South Deerfield in the form of a white elderly Christian gentleman, Woodfrey, and his doting wife, Eleanor, that the children affectionately called Grandpa Woody and Grandma Eleanor.

"You kids be good for your Grandpa Woody, you hear me?" Rose called from the front seat to the back of the car, her book bag balancing on her lap.

Onyii, Emeka, and Nate rode along in the backseat of Grandpa Woody's car. Strapped into the seatbelts that were anchored in the folds of the deep bucket seats, they could barely see out of the back windows of the car. As they arched their necks to look for familiar sights, they recognized the red brick buildings that comprised the Greenfield Community College where Rose had begun taking small evening courses. Apollos was also at school, so Grandpa Woody watched the children. He rolled the car up to the front door of the main building, and Rose turned around.

"You hear me?" she called over her shoulder. "You kids be good, and don't give Grandpa Woody any trouble. And, Onyii, you help take care of your brothers, okay?" The kids nodded in silent consent. Satisfied with this, Rose opened the door and stepped out of the car.

"We'll see you in a few hours!" Grandpa Woody cheerfully called out from the driver's seat.

As the car rolled away from the community college parking lot, the kids arched their necks to a final glance at their mother who was off to class; however, they were not sad because the fun was just about to begin. As they turned onto the main road, they exchanged looks with each other and smiled.

As the car pulled up to Grandpa Woody's colonial era house, the kids became antsy with anticipation and couldn't wait to go inside. At Grandpa Woody's house, they would eat cookies and then play with their grandpa all night long until it was time to go pick up their mother from school and go home.

This was a routine that they continued for years. It never dawned on them that Grandpa Woody was not their blood family; as soon as they saw him, they would bolt for him and take a running leap into his arms, crying with glee, "Grandpa Woody! Grandpa Woody!" They'd just assumed that he was a part of their family; though they knew he looked different, they had not quite pinpointed how he was related.

"Grandpa Woody was our very first grandpa! I think he was just fascinated by this African family, and he totally took us under his wing and watched over us, pretty much adopting us. We used to go over his house all the time, and I remember that I used to be *so* happy to see him whenever I saw him!" remembers Onyii.

Life for the Ihedigbos became pretty normalized fairly quickly. Apollos settled into his studies at the University of Massachusetts (UMass) while Rose studied at Greenfield Community College. The children enjoyed their new neighborhood, and between jumping around on their yellowish beige couch that served as the centerpiece of the living room and running around like kids do in the first large lush, grassy lawn they'd ever had, for them, life was good. The children would play outside under the bright Massachusetts sun with their very American friends, African and white mainstream friends sharing in games and fun together. Through these influences, the Ihedigbo children came to pick up more Westernized, mainstream ways of their own.

Onyii recalls her childhood neighbors, twins named Jennifer and Janelle. "Our house was next to theirs, and we played *all* the time—every day! Though we were African and clearly different from them, neither they nor their family ever treated us any differently."

While the Ihedigbos were warmly embraced by their new neighbors, Apollos and Rose remained watchful over their children, especially their daughter Onyii. As the eldest child and only daughter, her parents protected her from many things that they allowed her siblings to easily enjoy. For example, as friendly as they were, Onyii would have no sleepovers with Jennifer and Janelle—or anyone for that matter—ever. Even as she grew older, there would be no going to movies or attending parties with her friends. Apollos and Rose were diligent in their pursuits to protect and shield their daughter from becoming engaged in these things, a fact that they would openly acknowledge and still do not apologize for to this day. Some things are so special that they merit such protection.

The family was also immediately embraced by their new church home, North Leverett Baptist Church located in Leverett, Massachusetts, the church that Grandpa Woody and Grandma Eleanor attended as well. One of Apollos's advisors at UMass, also a Christian brother, had introduced them to the church, and the family enjoyed their new ministry home. Membership also had its benefits, for when the family needed a doctor for the children, they found one at North Leverett. Dr. Clapp, a member of the church who also worked at UMass Health Services, was very helpful in making sure that all of the Ihedigbo children were examined, treated, and that they remained healthy. Apollos and Rose were again grateful to God that He had provided for them in such a wonderful way. It was here at the North Leverett Baptist Church that the family remained until they eventually transitioned to College Church.

By the time the Ihedigbos had arrived here in South Deerfield, Massachusetts, they had become much more adept at fitting into the American culture that surrounded them. They had learned some American slang and knew how to converse about the weather, the news, and food. They knew what types of clothes to wear in certain types of weather. After their two years inter- acting with students and professors at Houghton, they began to understand American intonations and had adjusted their British intonations accordingly in order to be understood.

There was one thing, however, that remained peculiar to them, even two years after arriving in America; for the life of them, they could not understand why Americans speak so *softly*! To Apollos and Rose, it sounded almost as if Americans spoke in a loud whisper, and in order to figure out what they were saying, their eyes had to be fixated upon the mouths of the speakers and the movement of their lips. This was one American challenge they had not yet overcome, but other than this, things had started to fall into place.

The family's move for Apollos to attend the University of Massachusetts was, in many respects, different from their life at Houghton in New York. For starters, while they lived rent free in New York, in Massachusetts, they had to pay rent for their hous- ing. Then because everything was not within walking distance as in New York, Apollos and Rose had to learn the bus schedules so that they could navigate the transportation system and reach places like the grocery store.

In light of the additional expenses of living that they'd encountered in this next phase of the pursuit of their dream, Apollos and Rose made the necessary adjustments. For example, though they had four small children now, daycare was out of the question. In fact, none of the children received care outside of the home, with the exception of their time with Grandpa Woody and Grandma Eleanor, until they reached kindergarten age—because kindergarten was free.

Apollos delighted in taking classes at the University of Massachusetts. The beautiful green campus speckled with trees of brown, yellow, and orange hues along winding sidewalks that wove between the tall, strong, stately buildings gave him a sense of strength and pride. He was a master's student studying at one of the best institutions in one of the best nations in the world, second to his own homeland, of course. With a voracious appetite for learning, he absorbed every word he learned from every course in every classroom in which he sat, jotting down notes in his excellent penmanship that he would study later at home. At the next meeting of the course, he would ask questions that arose during his review of his study notes or his heavy textbook reading; Apollos Ihedigbo did not take education lightly, and he always came to class prepared.

The process of becoming thoroughly prepared each time Apollos took his seat at his desk was no small feat for someone in his position. As a family man, he had to make his presence felt with his loved ones, so in the midst of his busy schedule, he would take his family out to ride bicycles in the community, even though he was not much of an outdoor person; he'd rather be inside, as he was more of a homebody. The family also loved playing tennis. Apollos, Rose and the children all had their own rackets, and being such a fun and (best of all) free activity, it was one in which they engaged often. Apollos made sure that his presence was felt among his family members through outings like these.

Between being a supportive father who watched over his children while his wife was taking classes, to providing for his family of six (James had not been born yet) by taking every odd job that could accommodate his schedule—including pizza delivery man and custodian, to being a good husband and spiritual leader for the household, Apollos had to make strategic use of every moment of his "free time" in order to show up for his classes thoroughly prepared.

Apollos' diligence eventually paid off. On May 30, 1982, he graduated from the University of Massachusetts with a Masters in Education, and on May 23, 1987, he realized his dream of earning a doctorate in education.

Fortunately for Apollos, by the time he reached the doctoral level of his studies, he had reestablished contact with his dear friend Daniel Okorafor with whom he had attended teacher-training college in Nigeria. Like Apollos, Daniel had also traveled to the U.S. to pursue greater academic opportunities as well as business. After studying economics as an undergraduate and then moving into marketing management for his MBA, he joined Apollos in his program at the University of Massachusetts in Amherst for his doctoral studies, and they proudly graduated together from the same program at the same time.

In the meantime, while Apollos enjoyed his time on the UMass campus, Rose was completing her two-year liberal arts program at Greenfield Community College. The successful accomplishment of this program, when combined with the five courses she'd completed at Houghton, made her eligible to complete her bachelor's degree at UMass. She was proud to be enrolled in the prestigious academy along with her husband and had dreams of becoming an instructor, administrator, or trainer. To this end, she took classes to complete her bachelor's degree through the university's continuing education program, which meant taking most all of her courses in the evening. Without a break in enrollment, Rose would go on to complete not only her bachelor's degree in 1985, but a master's degree in 1986 and her doctorate in 1992, all in early childhood education.

During their time at UMass, Rose and Apollos learned and discovered many things. Outside of their degrees, however, one of the most significant they learned was how fulfilling it was to share the love of Christ abroad on the campus of the University of Massachusetts. This they did by leading and establishing their very own Bible study.

The First Baptist Church on the campus of the University of Massachusetts is a beautiful facility, the perfect backdrop for a groundbreaking Bible study developed by the Ihedigbos to shake the world for Christ. The small, modest group did not utilize the actual sanctuary; no, the gathering was much too small for this. Instead, a medium-sized classroom to the right of the church's entry housed the humble, spiritually-determined group once a week for prayer, encouragement, and study of the Bible.

The furnishing of this cozy, quaint space was sparse, featuring only chairs that outlined the perimeter of the room. Every Wednesday and Sunday evening, an evenly blended multicultural group of Americans and Nigerians—although more Nigerians than Americans—would trickle into the room and fill about twelve of the seats, talking in hushed voices that recounted the activities of their day to one another until it was time for the Bible study to begin.

"How was your day?"

"Oh, it was wonderful. Restful! How was yours?"

"I was finally able to phone my brother in Nigeria this morning, and he was telling me that one of my aunties in the village has fallen ill and has been taken to the hospital. Please be in prayer for my family."

"I and my family will most certainly will pray. I'll also make sure that Dr. Apollos remembers you for special prayer at the end of Bible study. Be encouraged, my brother. Our God is still in the healing business!"

At that, the elder statesman, Dr. Apollos Ihedigbo would begin the Bible study, leading his small but faithful group in singing songs of praise followed by taking turns reading through scripture.

"Verse 26: 'Likewise the Spirit also helps in our weaknesses. For we do not know what we should pray for as we ought, but the Spirit Himself makes intercession for us with groanings which cannot be uttered,'" someone would read with a thick Nigerian accent.

"Verse 27: 'Now He who searches the hearts knows what the mind of the Spirit *is,* because He makes intercession for the saints according to *the will of* God,'" another member of the group, a graduate student attending UMass from New York, would pick up in a sharp East Coast accent.

The readers would continue around the circle reading one verse each until each of the verses in the Scripture designated by Dr. Apollos for the discussion had been covered. After this, a lively and interactive discussion ensued as group members chimed in with their thoughts and opinions about the evening's lesson.

Once Dr. Apollos was able to corral the group and bring the discussion to a proper close, the group would end with prayer, making sure to lift up the special prayer needs of those in attendance.

"Pray that my cousin receives his visa to come to the United States to study. This is his fourth time trying, and we are believing God that this will be the time he will make it."

"Please pray for my family's need. We have not been able to find proper work yet, and it is difficult making ends meet."

"Please pray for my auntie in Nigeria. She fell ill in the village and has been taken to the hospital. The family is trying to put together money to get the hospital the medicine she needs."

"I would like to request prayer for my niece. She has one more year left in her secondary school but the corrupt records department is withholding her ability to register until her family pays them more money on the side."

All prayer requests spoken, Dr. Apollos would pray with fiery passion, mustering every bit of faith that resided in his spirit to believe that God would meet every need that had been voiced in the prayer circle as well as those that he knew had not been voiced. Spoken or not, when he finished his prayer, he was convinced that he had touched heaven and the heart of God, and every request that was made was already done.

Immediately following the closing prayer, the group would stand around for a few minutes of fellowship, especially if the Bible-study discussion had been particularly lively, to continue sharing their thoughts and ideas on the matter. If a member of the group was experiencing a particularly challenging financial need, the group would take up a collection for him or her to help get them through.

On certain special days a relative of the Ihedigbos would make delicious refreshments to share during the time of fellowship. The presence of such goodies made the children, who were occasionally dragged along to attend the group by their parents, especially happy to have endured the evening.

While the group bore no resemblance to the mega churches that pervade the Christian landscape today, the genuine, sincere desire to help others grow and develop in a pure, intimate relationship with God, the few faith-filled believers on hand was no less powerful, no less significant, and no less pleasing to God the Father than the vast multitudes that gather around the world for the same purpose.

In the end, the outcome was reached: each Wednesday and Sunday evening, the faithful group would leave the Ihedigbo Bible study, hearts aflame, passionate about their Lord, grateful that God had brought them together for a time of community, fellowship, sharing, and encouragement. They were family unified not by the blood that ran through their veins, but the blood that covered them in the sacrifice of Jesus Christ.

Any non-Nigerian who attended the African Christian Fellowship Bible study not only received an education on the Word of God, the fortunate attendee also received a bonus: an education on the rich cultural heritage of his hosts. By making repeated visits to fellowship with this dedicated group of Christians on the UMass campus, one could gain more insight into Nigerian culture in a few weeks than would be possible to learn in a classroom over the course of a semester.

Although the bulk of the participants were Nigerians, it was a very welcoming group that embraced those of other cultures and eagerly accepted them into their fold. In fact, it was not unusual for the group to, with great patience, teach their non-Nigerian guests Christian songs, words, and phrases in their native language. Over time, it was common for guests to report that they almost began to feel like they were Nigerian themselves!

AFRICAN CHRISTIAN FELLOWSHIP: CELEBRATIONS OF CHRIST AND CULTURE

"Hold that dish with a towel because it's hot, and I don't want you to drop it!" Rose would excitedly call out to her son who was loading up the minivan with mounds of slow-cooked Nigerian goodies. James and his friend Ike carefully, slowly carried the heavy treasures from the house outside to the waiting vehicle. Rose, Apollos, James, and James's best friend, Ike, were always in charge of transporting the food and drinks.

Huge pans of food covered every possible space on the minivan's floor, including fufu, rice dishes, soups, stews, and more, all made with love in the Ihedigbo kitchen and carefully covered with shiny foil so as not to spill their juices en route to their destination. The succulent cuisine could be for a graduation party, a wedding reception, a birthday gathering, a holiday, or for no particular reason at all on a sunny Saturday afternoon; the Nigerians just loved to gather. And why would they not? These events that they celebrated Nigerian style with their fellow expats helped to heal them from the daily stresses of being considered an alien in a foreign land and insulated them from the threats and dangers of being different in a society that has a hard time valuing those who do not look and act like "regular Americans."

These delicacies, however, were for a meeting of the African Christian Fellowship. As they walked over to the food table with their dishes, they noticed that the huge room was already filled with the smell of curry and onions. Besides their own, dish after dish was carried in what seemed to be a never-ending procession from their temporary holding places, nestled in the trunks of cars and the back rows of minivans and station wagons—dishes that were covered in foil and that had been simmering for hours until they were just perfect for the waiting African crowd that would soon devour it.

Milling around inside, the room was already getting loud. Nigerians sporting outfits made of busy, colorful fabric milled throughout the room. Hundreds of Nigerian women proudly donned their best African traditional dress, painstakingly sown by hand and tailored perfectly for their matronly frames. Elaborately tied headpieces adorned their heads as crowns, identifying them as the African queens they believed themselves to be—and indeed they were.

Around the large meeting hall, small children playfully darted in and out of the large crowd of their "aunties" and "uncles," fellow Nigerians who, though not related by blood, were just as much family to them as those with whom they shared actual biological ties. Older children in more Western attire congregated in distinct small groups around the perimeter of the room, taking in the sights and sounds of their elders who fellowshipped and socialized with one another, as was the African custom at these events.

This was a meeting of the African Christian Fellowship in Massachusetts, and African believers looked forward to such events all year. Nigerians from all over the region would pack up their families and make the pilgrimage to attend these fellowship gatherings as a means of worshipping together, staying connected to their people, and preserving cultural rituals. Meeting up with other Nigerians to catch up on the latest news from their homeland, sharing reports of the recent accomplishments of their children, and sharing testimonies of God's goodness with others who understood and appreciated their Nigerian culture made these events ones that could not be missed!

African Christian Fellowship (ACF) is a community organization that organizes leadership training and national and regional conferences and workshops to promote Christian values; it is also an organization upon which the Ihedigbos made their mark in Massachusetts.

While they attended UMass together, Apollos and Rose often got together with other Nigerians, families she and her husband had known back in Nigeria from Scripture Union. Rotating the meetings between Rose and Apollos's home and those of other group members, they fellowshipped, held meetings, sang songs, and worshipped the Lord; though their gatherings were loosely structured and informal, they just enjoyed the unity and camaraderie that coming together offered.

The value that surrounded the sense of sharing, comfort, and similarity of background was one that could not be underestimated. Each man, woman, boy, and girl who attended the group realized it—it was undeniably a significant part of their lives and helped to make it easier to cope in a foreign land. Understanding this, Apollos and Rose tried to include as many people as possible in their new group. Some Nigerians, they met through the UMass International Office. When new students come to the campus and ask university officials if there were any other Nigerians in the area, the office would immediately introduce the student to them. Word soon quickly spread around campus about the group of Nigerians that were organizing themselves on the campus.

Focused on more than just fellowship, they were there to help their brothers and sisters. When new Nigerian students came to campus, the group would go and visit them. Whatever the new students needed, the group provided, including providing groceries, sharing meals together, inviting them over for fellowship, and mentoring. As word continued to spread about the group of Nigerians, one of the Nigerian professors and a number of Nigerian professionals from the western Massachusetts area even joined. Together, they gathered over a potluck meeting once a month in someone's home, encouraging one another, sharing traditional food with one another, sharing news of what was happening back home, and making plans on how they would eventually return and touch Nigeria. To maintain close ties with their heritage, they would also gather to celebrate Nigerian Independence Day and host cultural shows that included showcases of Nigerian culture and fashion to educate others on traditions and their way of life.

On one occasion, this close Nigerian group was invited to attend a conference called the African Christian Fellowship by some of their brothers and sisters who were familiar with the organization and attended its events. Always looking forward to fellowship with other Nigerians, several members of the group attended the conference, which was being held in New York. After seeing ACF in action, Apollos and Rose instantly decided that this was exactly what they needed in Amherst; they would start a chapter of their own once they returned home. Being affiliated with such an organization would be a good way to strengthen relationships and provide fellowship for people like them who needed to spend quality time with Christian brothers and sisters, they decided. Since they were already having meetings anyway, they decided to make it official.

In 1996, the Ihedigbos filed their paperwork with the national chapter of the African Christian Fellowship to become recognized as a new, official chapter in Amherst, and after about six months of meeting and waiting, ACF of Amherst, Massachusetts, was born. Rose served as the president of ACF in Amherst, Massachusetts, for a number of years. This was a role that she took very seriously, scheduling who would lead the Bible study lesson, planning meetings, and getting the word out about upcoming gatherings and events to the group members.

Once the fellowship group had been formalized and the chapter established, they chose to move the meetings out of the individual homes to the Amherst Baptist Church, not far from the UMass campus. Each time they joined in with each other over singing, dancing, clapping, and fellowshipping, it felt like they'd brought a piece of Nigeria to the U.S.

ACF was no ordinary mainstream organization; it fellowshipped the Nigerian way. Each time a meeting was called, its guests became excited about what lay ahead: wearing their ornate African clothes, eating *moi moi*, Joloff rice, and plantain, and doing all of the things that marked the unique, specific way of Nigerian fellowship. After they had completed all of the items on their meeting agenda, including prayer, singing praises, and either a Bible story or a preached message, and then reception, they felt as if they were continuing the Scripture Union meetings of their youth right there in Massachusetts.

As ACF Amherst meetings grew, so did their purpose. Ultimately, the purpose was for fellowship; however, this was a time that preceded the Internet, so one of the most important aspects of the meeting was information sharing. Any person who had traveled to or received a letter from Africa would provide the group with updates of what was going on in their native land.

Another purpose that the ACF served was to identify those who could make special deliveries to loved ones when they returned to Nigeria for a visit. For example, if someone announced that he or she was planning a trip home, group members would begin writing letters to be delivered to their villages in addition to bringing mini care packages to be delivered. These packages might include toothpaste, toothbrushes, medicines, lotions, aspirin, soap, sanitary items, granola bars, M&M's, and any other goodies that are in scarce supply in a place like Nigeria. Their brothers and sisters back home loved American toiletries because that which is sold in Nigeria is not of the same quality as they could get in the States.

As many of these care packages as the group member was willing to carry were delivered to him, and he carefully identified a spot for each one of them in his baggage, recognizing that these goodies were more valuable than their material contents would suggest. They were not simply toiletries; they represented a message, a connection to the people they loved most in the world that said, "I am mindful of you!" With each delivery he dropped off on Nigerian soil, he would pick up a neatly handwritten letter to take back to their loved ones who eagerly anticipated his return back in the states.

Letters mailed from the East Coast of the U.S. to Nigeria typically took a month or two for the recipient to receive in the 1980s and 1990s. It was for this reason that when travelers were headed to their homeland, fellow Nigerians would jump at the opportunity to have them deliver a letter on their behalf.

Most of the group members who had come from Nigeria to live in the U.S. did not communicate with their loved ones by phone very often, and visits were even scarcer. Rose herself neither called home frequently, nor did she even return for a visit until after ten years of living in the United States. After all, making long-distance phone calls from the U.S. to Nigeria was quite expensive, and it was downright out of the budget when considering her and Apollos's limited finances as full-time college students with five kids. It was only after about ten years of being away from home that the two were able to call home every month or so using phone cards. By this time, they had completed much of their education, gotten jobs, and were better established. Years after this, the Internet made communication with their families back home much easier, but in the meantime, the trips that ACF members took comprised the extent of their information highway.

✤

While she was president of ACF Amherst, Rose had the opportunity to run her leg of the information superhighway, choosing to visit Nigeria for the first time after being away for ten years. The year was 1990, and on this trip, she traveled alone, letters and care packages from her ACF brothers and sisters in tow. The purpose of her trip was to visit her mother and her old friends.

As Rose encountered person after person desperate to travel to America to study, she again realized how privileged and fortunate she was. She felt blessed all over again to enjoy such a glamorous opportunity. In fact, the mere fact that she lived and studied in America made her an instant celebrity in the village. In any case, Rose did not allow this attention to go to her head. She knew that it could not have happened without Apollos and without her relationship with Christ. "In my most remote dreams," she says, "it would not have happened without God doing it."

Though she could not grant every request made of her on the trip, especially those for money and for her to take their children back with her on the plane so they could study in the U.S., Rose knew never to come to Nigeria empty-handed. Thus, along with the letters and small care packages that she brought back from her fellow ACF members, Rose brought gently worn extra clothing that she'd picked up from various clothing store and from her kids' closets. To this day, she remembers the level of gratitude they expressed at her kind gifts.

"People loved and cherished the clothing I brought with me from the U.S., some of them literally did not have anything on their backs, so they loved when we gave them our extra clothes. Even giving them one bar of soap was cherished so greatly, they instantly loved and valued any gift you could give them. It's still like that today. Poverty is so rampant. It makes me want to do more and more to help my people."

Rose sat close to her mother on the old, familiar couch. That was her mother's favorite couch, the one that held her "spot," her favorite place to sit in her house. Here, she could see everything that was happening in the house and outside in the compound at the same time. It was also here that she caught the coolest-possible breeze as it wafted across the linoleum-covered cement floor; it was the "sweet spot" of the house. While there were four sofas situated around the large living room of this flat five-bedroom house built by her father before he passed away, this one was the most comfortable. On it they sat together to catch up on ten years of growth and life changes.

"This is a picture of Onyii, Mama." She pointed out as she proudly handed over the photo with a big smile. Her eldest daughter had only been three years old when they'd left Nigeria, and now here was a picture of her thirteen-year-old Onyii, a young woman with a bright smile and a visibly brighter spirit.

"Oh my!" her mother exclaimed. "She's so big now! She looks just like you, Ijeoma! Look at that smile!"

"And here, these are pictures of the boys. This is Emeka. He's twelve now. Here is Nathaniel. He's eleven. And here are pictures of David and James. You've never seen them before. They are nine and six." With each new description of her boys, Rose handed her mother a few new photos. She watched as her mother considered her grandchildren carefully, a wide smile growing across her face. Even she was proud of her daughter's beautiful family.

"These are beautiful children, Ijeoma. Just beautiful," she said as she stared at each photo intently. "Everyone looks very healthy and very happy," she commented.

"We are, Mama. We are very healthy and happy, the Lord is providing for us, and Apollos is taking great care of us," Rose offered.

Rose went on to tell her mother about life in America, a topic that seemed to fascinate her to no end. She told her about school, about African Christian Fellowship, and about life in general. When her sister, Mary Akumah, and her family, who were visiting at the time, and Apollos's family members came to visit, she prepared herself to repeat the same stories. Everyone wanted to know what life was *really* like in America, and after ten years of being away, she was ready with a good report.

As Rose lay down in the small bedroom at the end of the day, she felt genuinely blessed. She'd told the story of how blessed her life was so many times to so many people that day; she had even been reminded about how privileged she was. In the room next door, she heard a pastor rustling around, probably pulling up a chair to the small table to study his Scriptures under the light of the lamp. Her mother would often allow pastors and ministers to occupy her spare bedrooms and to stay as long as they wanted to stay. At this, Rose began to thank God for the seeds of a relationship with Christ that her mother had planted in her as a young child, seeds which sprang forth in a true, intimate, and fruitful relationship with Christ, allowing her to touch the lives of others with His love in a very real way. The thought of this brought tears to her eyes.

Two weeks later, Rose ended her visit with letters for her friends carefully packed away in her carry-on baggage. It was time to return to her new home to continue her work of ministry with the African Christian Fellowship.

One of the benefits of being an official ACF chapter is that the local chapter has the privilege to host a weekend conference of its own. The Amherst chapter looked forward to arranging such an important event, and the opportunity to host its very own conference overwhelmed them with excitement. These conferences were a family affair that reinforced everything the Nigerians knew and loved about their culture.

Rose recalled how proud she and Apollos were to host ACF Amherst's first official chapter conference.

"It was a Sunday evening event held at the UMass Baptist Church. We were so very happy and proud because it was such a joyous occasion! We had our Christian brothers and sisters from Boston, New York, Philadelphia, and all across the East Coast there to support us! It was so beautiful and glorious that the people from Boston who came down went back to Boston and started their own chapter! Like us, they had been meeting but were not formally an ACF chapter. We were very proud that visiting us motivated them to start ACF Boston!"

After the ceremonial passing around of a kola nut and peanut butter, the festivities kick into high gear as the music begins, and hundreds of Nigerians and guests converge upon a dance floor to dance the evening away. All who attended the African Christian Fellowship conferences knew that they were in for a good time—including their American guests.

Esther, an American guest and good friend that the family invited to the ACF conference, remembered the fun that she would have with Rose at the events.

"Rose is balanced—she's very spiritual, but she's also a lot of fun. She *loves* to dance and have a good time! Of course, I was American, so American dancing was all I knew, but the way Rose started dancing was just so cute that I wanted to learn! She taught me some African dances, and after a while, the Nigerian men and women would come out with their brightly colored, elaborate African garb and masks. The ladies would do their dances like fancy birds, and they wore fancy hats made with large pieces of brilliant, bright starched material. Together, they would dance while we stood on the sides and watched, dancing along ourselves. It was something to see! I would be thinking to myself, 'Wow…this is so…rich!' The only parties I was familiar with were American ones where people get intoxicated, dance with you, and try to take you home for sex the same night. Here, there was none of that—just community, fun, celebration, and love among brothers and sisters."

The Ihedigbos loved these times of community, culture, and fellowship with their fellow African brothers and sisters because events like these kept them intimately and actively tied to the rich culture and heritage with other believers that defined the essence of who they were.

US-born African-Americans have asked on occasion why an organization like this—one that brings people together for fellowship—is necessary. The answer to such a question is a complex one because it taps into issues deeper than meet the eye.

A peculiar thing tends to happen in the minds of African-Americans who have been born and reared in the United States with no knowledge of their African ancestry. If perchance they have the opportunity to encounter large groups of Africans either on African or American soil, they are faced with negotiating a psychological dilemma. When witnessing the pride, the unity, and the strength of Africans—pure Africans whose rich African blood has not been diluted and whose psyches have not been broken or beaten into complacency through hundreds of years of being subjected to an unjust, oppressive slavery system—African-Americans often report experiencing a sense of feeling robbed of a life that could have been. The solidarity, the sense of efficacy, and the high sense of esteem and confidence that Africans feel—often referred to as African swagger and misinterpreted as African arrogance—is markedly different from what the typical African-American is socialized to feel when growing up in the context of a country that has subjected the race to oppression for so many years.

Passed down through the DNA of African-American ancestors are certain psychological markers that tend to keep members of this group "in their place" feeling exactly the opposite of what native Africans exude as an ethnic group. As a result, when African-Americans are allowed the opportunity to witness the tremendous sense of pride and confidence that Africans possess, it is not uncommon for them to wonder what their lives might have been like—what they would have been able to accomplish in life—had they been raised in a context in which they were nurtured to believe that they were the most intelligent, innovative, wise, spiritual, and capable people on God's earth. There is an undeniable sense of envy that naturally arises in African-Americans when they sit back to witness the natural swagger of their African brothers and sisters. It is this confidence, this sense of capability, this pride, that carries Nigerians ahead, doing great things for their families and their country—including the Ihedigbos.

IT TAKES A VILLAGE: YOUTH SHENANIGANS, DISCIPLINE, AND A FATHER'S LOVE

Nathaniel (Nate) Ihedigbo's earliest childhood memory is one of him standing, mouth agape, in the living room of the Ihedigbo family's modest apartment in Amherst, witnessing one of the most remarkable sights he'd ever seen in his short life—a large solid white snowdrift that was so high it reached over the top of the front door of the first-floor residence, apartment J-1. Winters were snowy in Massachusetts; and because the entrance of the apartments—arranged into quads—faced a corridor, each time the Eastern snow fell, huge pileups of white powdery snow in front of the door were inevitable. Fortunately, residents had back doors that led to backyards that connected to one another, and they could escape their snowed-in confines through this alternate route.

Days like these were not sad, stressful ones; in fact, quite the opposite is true. Days like these allowed the Ihedigbos to do more of what they loved most: spend time with the family in their warm, cozy home sharing stories, humor, and wisdom that would carry the children through life, helping them to avoid as much harm as possible. The happy-face-shaped gutters that surrounded the North Village Apartments were a telltale sign of what the complex represented in the simple yet contented lives of its residents.

This apartment served as the backdrop for many fond Ihedigbo memories. The boys slept in one room while Onyii had her own room—a privilege she'd always enjoyed as a result of being the only girl in the family—and Mom and Dad shared the largest of the rooms. Whether playing lively, spirited games with one another in their rooms or riding bikes, be it their own or one of the "neighborhood bikes" that all the kids in the community shared, the close-knit family of Nigerians learned to enjoy life wherever they were in, including the tight confines of a family of seven squeezed into a three-bedroom apartment.

The Ihedigbos had located these small yet comfortable quarters not through a realtor or an ad in the local newspaper but through the same means that Nigerians locate most of the knowledge and resources they acquire—the Nigerian network. In the case of this dwelling, Apollos and Rose had received a referral from the network and found it a suitable place to live. There was also an added benefit to living here, as Rose worked at the daycare center located on the apartment premises. As there were many immigrant student parents living in the apartment complex, their children attended the daycare center where Rose worked as well.

From New York, the Ihedigbos had moved into this town where people measured their position, status, and importance in life by where they lived, what they wore and what they drove; the Ihedigbos would have been considered to be at the bottom of the totem pole—last in the pecking order. However, the children were well insulated from this knowledge. "We didn't know we didn't have a lot," Nate explains. "We had family, and that was plenty."

In Nigerian culture, people from the same culture and especially those who are from the same village are called auntie and uncle and their children are called cousins. "We had several cousins who lived in the same apartment complex, and that helped to make it fun," Nate remembered, reflecting on the good times he had with his cousins Gracious and Jonathan who were one of several of the family's African neighbors.

Together with their cousins, the friends they made in the apartment complex, and the classmates that they shared most of their days with at Marks Meadow Elementary, the young

Ihedigbos found means to entertain themselves in ways that cost them no money but that did require loads of innovation. For example, one of their favorite pastimes involved a red wheelbarrow, toads, and a few makeshift weapons—an unlikely combination for the unimaginative mind, but a formula for hours upon hours of fun for the Ihedigbos.

It would be impossible to imagine the number of ways that a group of children could entertain themselves for days on end with a simple wheelbarrow, but Emeka, Nate, David and James found a way. In addition to finding a way, they found toads in the apartment's gutters, lots and lots of toads, as they were plentiful and powerless against the creative schemes of the boys, who would load them up in the wheelbarrow and have their way with them.

During those days of the early '80s, Apollos and Rose were constantly engaged in the pursuit of their goals to build a better life for their children. As a result, Apollos was most often either working or studying and Rose was away taking classes at school. The absence of having both parents at home during strategic hours of the day gave the Ihedigbo kids, particularly the sons, a prime opportunity to engage in the mischief that went hand in hand with being boys.

The telephone rang on the other end as Nate, Emeka, and David all huddled around the receiver to listen. James was only six years old. "Amherst Fire Department," the person on the other end answered.

"Um...we have a...um... fire," Nate said.

"You have a fire? Is this real, or are you playing on the phone?" the firehouse operator asked.

"Uh...we have a fire," Nate repeated, barely able to stifle his giggles or those of his brothers who listened in.

"Is there an adult there with you?" the operator asked. "What are you doing home unsupervised without a guardian?"

At that, the boys hung up the phone. They'd only meant to play a little joke on the local fire department, not to potentially get their parents in trouble, their parents who were out working hard to build the American dream so they could have a better life. They were instantly terrified.

Within minutes, there was a loud pounding on the door. *Bam! Bam! Bam!* Onyii rushed to open the front door, and to her surprise, there stood three firemen dressed in gear.

"Hello, little girl. Is there an adult here with you?" the tall one asked.

"No, I'm here watching my four brothers," Onyii replied. She was only 14 years old.

The firemen stayed in front of apartment J-1 that day and would not leave until an adult came to the apartment to supervise the children at home alone. Fortunately, Auntie Bridget came over to the apartment relatively quickly because she lived in the same apartment complex.

After this incident, a variety of random aunties came to the Ihedigbo apartment to check on the children, bring them food, and ensure that they were taken care of. The rich soil of Nigeria is not the only place where a village can thrive. With the love and concern that they shared for one another's children and overall well-being, a true Nigerian village existed right in the middle of the North Village Apartments in Amherst, Massachusetts.

Mischief was par for the course when so many boys were left to their own devices while their busy parents spent day and night at school and work to build the foundation of a better life for their family. One memory engrained in David's memory occurred on one of such occasions when Mom and Dad were both away. By this time, David was in the sixth grade, and his brothers were older, capable of watching him and his little brother, James, the baby of the family.

"James, give it back *now*!" David shouted. James soared off the top of the bunk bed, darting through the room and out the door like a superhero. In his hand, he held his brother's prized possession. He knew that it rightfully belonged to David, but he'd wanted to see it. David was accustomed to sharing everything, but not this—this was his, and it was special. Thus, James decided to take things into his own hands.

"Give it back, James! I said give it back!" roared David as he ran in hot pursuit after his little brother. The more he ran, the quicker James became, darting in and out of rooms, up and down the stairs, over chairs, under tables, and around and around the couch. *This kid is fast*, David thought.

"No! Let me see it!" James called out behind his back, closely guarding the possession by holding it close to his body as his brother stayed on his heels. He was the baby of the family and thus entitled to the benefit of seeing such special things. No one, even his slightly older brother David, would deny him this privilege granted to him by birth order alone.

"James, when I catch you, I'm going to beat you up! I mean it!" David yelled as the chase continued. James and he would always bump heads for some reason or another, and this would always end up in a fight. *This time, James would be in for a real good pummeling*, thought David. That is if he could ever catch him.

Through the house they ran for what seemed like an eternity until both boys tired out and slowed down their pace. James could see that his brother would be relentless in recovering his possession, so he let David catch him. He was tired of running. As soon as he received this opportunity, onto James David leaped, driving James's back into the sofa. Fueled by his anger, he hit his little brother with the right fist, then the left, in a fast rotation that left his little brother crying for mercy. James fought back, but he was no match for his older brother, especially when he'd already exhausted so much energy sprinting through the house.

After successfully subduing his little brother and recovering his valuables, David went back to his room. By this time, his older brothers, Emeka and Nate, had come back into the house from playing outdoors.

"What just happened?" they asked. "Why are you breathing so hard?"

Assured that his brothers would understand his point of view in the matter, David went on to tell his brothers about the situation that they had just missed, including what David did and how he had just put a mild beating on his little brother. However, they were not so understanding. In fact, they turned on him!

In an instant, in what seemed like one fluid motion, Emeka and Nate picked David up, carried him to the couch in the family room, opened up the sofa bed, put David inside, folded the bed back up, replaced the sofa cushions, and stacked as much movable furniture as they could find on top to ensure that there was no escape. Here, in the Ihedigbo household, you didn't mess with the baby of the family.

Inside the sofa bed, David lay trapped while his brothers frolicked outside, riding their bikes throughout the neighborhood; despite his best efforts and his young strength, he could not escape! Fortunately, before long, his mother came home and, hearing David's muffled moans for help, freed her young son from the confinement of the family sofa.

Though they could not stop them altogether, to at least mitigate the frequency of the childhood antics and keep them from getting out of hand, Apollos and Rose measured out discipline as each situation called for it. Just like in any family, one parent is usually more of a disciplinarian than the other. In the Ihedigbo household, the primary disciplinarian was Mom. With a "bionic arm," she doled out slaps and spankings like speed lightning to keep her five children in line.

Children will always be children and try to push the envelope as far as they think it might go, testing the waters just to see what they can get away with. Sitting at the dinner table, if they would blow bubbles in their milk or sip their water a little more loudly than they should, they would offer a quick sideways glance in her direction to see if she was watching. She would indeed have her eyes planted on them and would meet their sideways gaze with one of her own which said, "You better stop that right now!" If the child ignored the message, quicker than the eye could see, their mother would hop up with superhuman speed, reach across the table, render a strong slap across the child's face, and then sit back down to her dinner of stew, yams, and rice. It all seemed to happen in less than a second with one fluid motion, leaving the offender rubbing his face. "Owwww!"

However, Dad operated in a different disciplinary fashion, using the Bible as his tool of choice, making the young offender hold his big, thick Bible in the air for a certain amount of time. If he allowed his arms to fall, he would have to start the time all over again. The situation was not made any easier by the other kids peeking around the corner, silently pointing, laughing, and making silly gestures at whatever child was holding the Bible with trembling arms on a given day. By the time they were done with such punishment, they would never commit the offense again.

Despite his use of God's word for disciplinary measures, Apollos was also not averse to the use of more corporal type of punishment: swinging a belt!

"Let's stop by the university store first, guys," Nate said to James and David as the young boys walked home from school on a cool, brisk day. Their father worked at the university, so they often went to the university store that was run by college students. As the boys walked up and down the familiar aisles, they noticed that the college student working the register was not paying any attention to them. In fact, he was wearing his headphones, eyes closed, and bobbing his head to the tunes that were pulsing through his ears. The boys looked at one another mischievously as they stood in front of the candy aisle and surveyed the range of delicious treats available.

Who the first person was to suggest that they stuff hoards of candy into David's backpack remains a mystery even to this day; however, in the end, the brothers left the store with enough candy to occupy their sweet tooth for quite sometime. When they entered the house, they made a beeline for the bedroom to split up the bounty between them. However, somehow, in what also remains a mystery even to this day, Dad found out about the candy and demanded that the backpack be brought out of hiding and set before him.

"Where did you get this candy?" he demanded of the small boys who stood before him, knees shaking at the prospect of their God-fearing, Bible-believing giant of a father finding out that they had actually resorted to something as immoral as stealing. No one wanted to speak. The unified silence of the young culprits infuriated Apollos even more.

Eventually, David decided to speak up and take one for the team, confessing that the plan was his idea and that the bag full of candy was his alone. Apollos would be sure to chastise this child in such a way that he would never consider laying hold to anything that did not belong to him ever again. Combining heavy, swift belt action that seemed like it would never end followed by his favorite Bible activity, David learned his unforgettable lesson. He would go on to never ever steal again.

At times, the siblings had fun at the expense of their father's disciplinary methods. As youngsters, they made up a game simply called daddy that all of the kids would play while Apollos was either away at one of several jobs or at school. In this game, one of the children was selected to be "Daddy." As soon as the game was in play, they would begin busily fiddling around and having a good time. Then "Daddy" would walk in from work or school. Instantly, all of the children had to fall down and immediately pretend they were asleep, being completely still. Whoever "Daddy" observed not being completely still would get "spanked" with a little rubber cane, a consequence that caused the offender to burst out in giggles instead of tears. Though the children made light of the discipline their father doled out, they knew it was a serious matter, and they did all they could to not be on the receiving end of it.

There were certain heightened levels of expectations placed on Emeka as the eldest son of the Ihedigbo clan, as placed on most boys that fall in this honored birth-order position—especially in an African family. Expected to watch out for his only sister and see after his little brothers, all while serving as the ideal example of how an Ihedigbo child was to behave was a daily pressure. Apollos was almost militaristic in his expectations of this particular son, often holding him to a higher level of accountability and discipline than the others because of the role he played in the family. This often led to violent explosions as the younger and older men collided. Over time, this took its toll on the young Ihedigbo who was in junior high school at the time.

"I can't take this anymore!" Emeka yelled as he ran out of the room, knowing he was spinning out of control as a range of intense emotions flooded over him. He had just been severely disciplined yet again by his father who had been very stern with him, and Emeka thought it unfair. He was doing all he knew to do, but the pressure to fulfill the role as the perfect elder son who did no wrong was wearing on him. He ran to his room where he collapsed on his bed, covering his face as he sobbed loudly and openly.

"I don't know what to do!" he cried as he rolled around on his bed sobbing. "I don't know how to get out of this situation! This is too much for me…I can't do it anymore," he moaned through body-retching sobs, his pillow drowning in desperate, hopeless tears.

After several minutes, his father came to the door. There his son lay in the most desperate, vulnerable state he had ever seen, eyes red and puffy and face soaked in tears. He slowly walked over to his son's bed and sat down on its edge.

"You know I love you more than anything in this world," Apollos said.

"I know, Dad," his son replied, his voice cracked and breaking from his intense emotional outpouring. Apollos turned and looked at his eldest son in the eyes.

"Emeka, I realize I am a little too hard on you," Apollos began. "Emeka, I prayed and prayed for the Lord to make a change in my behavior, and He has. From this day forward, I promise that I will never ever lay my hands on you again." True to his word, Apollos never did. Not once.

This would turn out to be one of the most moving, powerful experiences Emeka had ever shared with his father. It helped to frame his faith moving forward because he'd experienced right before his very eyes the power of God to change an individual. From the point of that conversation on, whenever it came time for discipline, his father was a different person. Each time, Emeka honored God for his power to change things.

STUMBLES ON THE SUCCESS JOURNEY: GROWING UP POOR AND THE SURVIVAL CENTER

Apollos and Rose's clan might not have had the finest brand-name labels in their wardrobes, the latest in electronics, or extra bills to spend frivolously on nights out with their upper middle-class friends, but they never went hungry. Apollos was nothing if not a strong provider, and though he could not always provide all of the trappings that his kids wanted when they saw them sported by other families in his middle class neighborhood, he always provided what they needed. The essentials were always present.

Rose browsed the sale racks at the local discount department store looking for a coat that would provide just the right combination of affordability, style, and functionality for her sons. The freezing weather was ruthless in the heart of the winter, and she wanted to ensure her children were well insulated against the biting cold, and when she found just the right jacket, she would buy the same jacket in three different sizes; the youngest, James, would have to wear his older brothers' hand-me-downs. She found one that looked ideal and held it up.

"How about this one? Do you like this?" Emeka, Nate, and David scrutinized the puffy winter coat that dangled in the air before them.

"It's okay," said Nate.

"I like it," said David.

"It's fine," said Emeka.

James looked on silently. He did not have a voice or a vote because he did not have a choice. He was the youngest son and the recipient of hoards of hand-me-downs from three older brothers who grew like weeds. Everything in his wardrobe had been previously worn, from his coats and hats to his jeans and undershirts—and yes, even his underwear. The fact that their little brother was the hand-me-down king was not one that escaped his brothers' ridicule, as they constantly ribbed James for his position in the family and the benefits it carried of always having plenty of clothes waiting to be passed down.

"That's just how things went growing up. I got the hand-me-downs. If there were ever clothes to be bought, I was always the last one. You get the butt end of the stick when you're the youngest of four boys, but that just comes with the territory, so I never really dreaded." Rather than resent the jokes or the ribbing, James recognized that getting picked on by his brothers was just the way it was—it was the normal way of expressing brotherly love.

Despite his position as the last in line to receive anything new in the family's pecking order, fate occasionally smiled on James in the form of his frugal father loosening the purse strings just enough to bring a huge smile to the face of one of his children.

"I was playing seventh and eighth grade basketball, and all of the kids on the team were buying the new Jordans or Nikes. I was like, 'Wow! I've got to get a fresh pair of kicks!'" However, James knew that in a family of seven with restricted resources, money was tight and his chances of getting his hands on a luxury like expensive name-brand shoes would take a miracle on the level of the opening of the Red Sea!

"Dad, can you please get me a new pair of shoes?" he asked, "I need them for basketball."

"What's wrong with the shoes you have already?" he asked.

James had anticipated this. "They're all worn out, and I need some more if I'm going to be able to play well like the other guys."

"Okay. We'll go get you some shoes," Apollos conceded. He knew his son was a natural athlete who loved basketball, and he could not very well play the game without the proper gear.

On a sunny afternoon, Apollos drove his youngest son to the shoe store. With his plan in mind, James had steered his father to the parking lot of the local shoe store that housed his desired prize: a pair of name-brand shoes. Project miracle was in action.

As they entered the store, James set off to find the perfect pair of shoes as his father browsed the wall display of every shape, color, and style of shoe imaginable. James soon returned with a pair of Jordans. These would go perfectly with his team uniform. "Can I have these, Dad?"

"How much are they?" Apollos asked in his thick Nigerian accent reserved for times when he was in passionate or protective defense mode.

"They're $80," James said without flinching. It was worth a try.

Apollos laughed. "There is no way that I will *ever* spend $80 on sneakers, and neither will you!" he said to James's disappointment. Then he held up a pair of shoes he'd been surveying. "How about these?" It was a pair of Converse that fastened with a strap instead of shoestrings. The most attractive aspect of them to Apollos: they were only $29.

"Dad, I'd rather quit basketball than wear those!" James objected. He then picked up another pair of shoes that he thought might stand a chance, a $50 pair of black-and-white Nikes. "What about these?"

"No!" his father exclaimed, "That's just too much for some shoes!" However, upon seeing the look of great disappointment on his son's face, he soon gave in, and James left the store with the first of what would be many pairs of top-brand shoes he would wear—and with a huge grin.

"My dad gave in, not because we could afford them, but out of his love for me. That's why he bought them, and I've never forgotten that," James recalls.

Onyii shares a similar story of cracking the safe of Fort Knox also known as her father's wallet. Her father was a very frugal man out of the sheer necessity of having seven mouths to feed, clothe, shelter, and sustain; however, his daughter was his beloved, and occasionally, she could get him to part with a little more than he'd intended on spending.

"When I was in seventh grade, I asked my dad for the Adidas soccer shoes with the long tongue. I wanted some so bad to wear with my jeans that were tapered at the bottom in those days."

"I already got you sneakers!" Apollos replied.

"But they're from K-Mart, Dad! K-Mart!" Onyii pleaded.

"We can't afford those shoes you want," her father would say. "Be thankful to God that you have the sneakers you have."

"And then," Onyii continues with a soft, fond smile of her father, "He took me to Footlocker—my very first time ever in that store—and bought me some Adidas. They were $30 bucks, and I was like '*Whoa!*' I was happy with the shoes, but my heart was even more filled with happiness that my dad loved me so much that he would do anything for me. He always wanted to see us happy."

Nate sat on the hard bench in the boys' locker room, clenching his gym bag tightly. He looked around to see who was watching as he slowly opened his gym bag and carefully began to remove his pants and take off his shirt. As he continued to change into his gym shorts, eyes darting back and forth to see who was peeking, each step of his undress revealed the hidden secrets that lay beneath his clothes.

The Ihedigbos were clearly Nigerian. The cold Massachusetts winters chilled them down to their sun-loving African cores, and it didn't take much for them to feel the bitter cold down in their bones, especially when the stinging Arctic wind blew hard against them. Like any good Nigerian parents, Apollos and Rose made every effort to protect their children, and this protection included insulation against the elements. Their solution to keeping their sons warm: thick, brilliant, emerald-green wool tights, and orange turtleneck dickies.

Once looking at the orange and green winter accessories with humiliation, Nate and his brothers now reflect upon them with hilarious laughter. "It was so cold in the winters that we would have to wear these green wool tights because as Nigerians, we were not used to the cold! It was so embarrassing going to gym in the first and second grade and having to take my tights off in front of the guys. No other kids wore tights besides me and my brothers. The other kids just wore jackets!" He also remembers the orange dickies with chuckles of the memory: "My parents would get us these turtlenecks with just the necks. It was so weird! It was orange with a flap in the front and a flap in the back, and all it had was a neck! We used to have to wear these under our clothes!" Today, the children reflect on these wardrobe staples that served as yet another way that made them different in school.

The journey from survival to success is one on which you are bound to meet the most helpful people and organizations on the planet—those that provide for just enough of what you need to survive right when you need it. One such organization that helped the Ihedigbos along their journey was the Survival Center, a place similar to the more well-known Salvation Army or Goodwill stores throughout the U.S. where those who were homeless or low or no income could come to receive clothes for their families free of charge. Sometimes there was even a little food to be scored.

The old red brick building that was attached on one side to a small house housed the Survival Center, which was not a far drive from the Ihedigbo home. Its parking lot was a long stretch of alley down, which those who were down on their luck in the pursuit of the American dream would walk or drive, actually looking forward to the warm, welcoming comfort and the friendly, smiling faces they would soon encounter in the store.

From the outside, stairs led visitors out of the biting cold or the blazing sun down into the always-comfortable aid center, with the descent finally landing them onto a well-worn hardwood floor filled with racks and racks of clothing donated by those more privileged; those whose children had grown out of their cute seasonal outfits, who had themselves overindulged and no longer fit into the clothes of their earlier years—after "saving" the clothes for several years, they'd finally conceded the battle of the bulge and donated them; those who enjoyed the excesses of life and shopped until their closets overflowed, making the donation of some of the "old" necessary in order to have more room "new"; and even those who'd dropped off a few select items in December simply for the purpose of getting a tax-deduction receipt before the new year. It was through these clothes and their makeshift handwritten labels that the Ihedigbos browsed several times a year to find clothes that would carry them through the next of Amherst's extreme seasons.

"We went to the Survival Center to get clothes so regularly that the people who worked there literally knew us by name," James recalls. "It was kind of like when a wealthy person walks into Saks Fifth Avenue and the managers and workers say, 'Hey, Mr. So and So. Nice to see you! I have some nice things I think you'd like to see.' Well, we would walk into the Survival Center and they would say, 'Hello, Mr. Apollos! How's it going? I see you brought the boys and your daughter with you today!" Then we would go through and pick out whatever clothes we needed for the season. We'd go often. It was how we survived."

When the children were very young, Apollos and Rose would comb through the racks, searching for comfortable clothes to suit each child; however, as they grew older, they took over this critical task, as their reputation at school depended heavily on the types of treasures they could find at the Survival Center, treasures that would allow them to blend in with their more affluent class-mates—or at least the middle-class ones.

Nate recalls that initially he was self-conscious and leery at the prospect of shopping for clothes in the Survival Center.

"Going to the Survival Center was embarrassing at first. When we first started going, I was like, 'All right, you guys can go. I'm just going to stay here in the car.' As we grew older, it was like a hustle. You could go and scrounge the racks and find something nice. Sometimes they even had brand-new stuff!" Nate remembers. He also recalls his sister, Onyii, the oldest of the brood who'd inherited her mother's creative, artistic expres-sion, showing her younger brothers that "free" did not necessarily mean "cheesy." It could mean fierce style.

"My sister kind of put us onto how to mix and match things from Survival Center so they would look good. She became a real artist at it. Onyii would always find all kinds of stuff and style them into a really cool outfit—kind of like vintage wear today. Her friends at school would always be like, 'Wow, Onyii! That is *hot*!' She helped us to see that there was a lot of good stuff in there if you take time to search."

Onyii owns being vintage before vintage was cool. "We took pride because no one else had the clothes we had. After we started wearing the vintage clothes, other people would want to go to second-hand stores to find the same things! 'Where can I find that stuff?' they would ask."

Once the Ihedigbos children really got the hang of shop-ping for used clothing, they ventured out; they would make trips to another Survival Center, one located in Hadley, to see what was new. "Hadley was a small town," Nate explains of making trips that took them beyond the closer Amherst location, "so we figured that they would have more available stuff." Not to mention, Nate fondly remembers that the center had "those big mega chocolate muffins there, which made it so cool to go there, because we got clothes *and* treats!"

When children are raised in a household filled with love, support, and vision for a greater future, the fact that they are living such a happy life below certain national income thresholds, like that which signifies low income, may elude them. Simply put, children may not come to the realization that their families have less than others do because in their minds, everyone is safe, comfortable, together, and happy—and that is all that matters. In such a context, they may not realize for quite some time that behind closed doors, they enjoy less in terms of luxury than their friends do. Such is the case for the Ihedigbos, who growing up, did not know that they were poor.

"It wasn't until I was eight or nine years old that I realized we were poor," recalls Onyii. "I realized it then because my mom always had to put stuff on layaway for us at K-Mart, and I always went somewhere else with my dad because I didn't want to be seen at the K-Mart."

Over the years, the family would realize that though they were poor in financial resources, their wealth overflowed with the things that really mattered: love, support, safety, and relationship with a God who supplied all of their needs, scarce as their resources were.

SIGNS OF A BRIGHTER FUTURE: LIFE IN THE SUBURBS OF AMHERST

The house at 29 Tamarack Drive in Amherst, Massachusetts, housed many of the earliest memories of the Ihedigbo children. This gray house with hints of blue was a two-story paradise in a new subdivision for the family that previously lived in the UMass university apartments. On the day the Nigerian family moved into the neighborhood, the day they carefully transported the meager goods that they had collected while they resided on the UMass campus, the house had four bedrooms and a gravel drive-way. However, these were the Ihedigbos whose leader Apollos was always improving, always advancing, always growing.

"The day we moved into our house on Tamarack Drive," Onyii recalls, "when we drove up to it, I remember feeling like 'Wow! We're like really middle class now! We're really normal now!' Not only were we the first Africans to move into this all-white neighborhood, we were the first blacks. I had my own room in a suburban neighborhood—I felt so special! This was the day I started feeling normal because prior to this, my brothers and I had always felt different or out of place. We all struggled with it at some level, but this move changed things for us."

Emeka also remembers the significance of purchasing a house like 29 Tamarack Drive. "The house on Tamarack was the embodiment of the American dream! After living in apartments for so many years, we finally owned our own home! Being able to say, 'Hey, this is ours!' was a significant moment for us."

Apollos nestled on his favorite spot on the family's comfortable sofa with his youngest son, James, at his side, casually enjoying the evening television network lineup. As he was giving his commentary on the last scene of the show before the commercial break, he stopped in midsentence at what he saw.

"Who needs a professional painter when you've got *this*! With the wave of one hand, you have one full coat of paint on the walls, and then you can get back to your weekend!" The commercial showed one of the most beautiful sights a do-it-yourselfer could ever hope for.

"Finish your painting in record time, all with the fast and easy flick of a wrist!" The commercial went on to show a high-pressure spray-painting machine whose ease and efficiency appeared to turn several days worth of painting into only hours. It was amazing to this elder Nigerian who was not one to want everything that he saw, but who—when he saw something he really wanted—had to have it, especially if it was for the family.

"We're getting *that*!" Apollos exclaimed! James, who knew that he would inevitably be a part of the painting crew, concurred; however, he noted there were things that arose after the fact that had not been considered.

"The commercial failed to mention how you had to plug your ears because the machine was *so* incredibly loud and so messy that it didn't even make sense! Dad made us get up on a ladder and made us paint away. It took us three weeks to get done, when it would have taken a contractor only one week to do. Fortunately, dad gave in and let a professional builder come to do the driveway." Apollos and his built-in labor force would go on to complete many do-it-yourself projects, and though the outcome was not always necessarily as precise as a professional contractor would have it, they got the job done.

"When we moved into the house, it had four bedrooms and a gravel driveway," recalls James. "By the time we moved out, it had seven bedrooms, a paved driveway, and it was completely repainted. It looked like a new house, and we did just about everything ourselves. After all, when you have four boys living in your house, you have an instant paint crew!" The Ihedigbos, as with everything they engaged in, started with the small and humble and put in the work to turn the house into their own beautiful masterpiece that was the envy of their neighbors—the typical Nigerian way.

Perhaps the biggest deal surrounding their move into the new home was the fact that all of the boys did not have to share one bedroom. "I would share with either David or James," Emeka explains, "and my other two brothers would share a room—but this did not last. Bedrooms changed with allegiances. We quickly turned into factions. I would partner up with James to go against the other two in whatever silly disagreement we would have. Then the next week, it was, 'You're not my roommate anymore!' and the rotation would begin again. It was like musical chairs!"

If the house at 29 Tamarack Drive suggested "normal American family," the purchase of the family's first minivan solidified it. "The minivan was created for us!" son Emeka says.

"One day, my dad said, 'I'm going to get a car for us.' He came back with a Dodge Caravan with a turbo engine in it! I was like, 'Dad! Where did you *find* this thing?'"

The family gained much use out of the minivan all over town and up and down the road when they went to visit aunts and uncles, attend conferences, or take family trips. As soon as one of the kids was old enough to drive, he was put behind the wheel to chauffeur the rest of the crew to its destination.

Wanting to experience the true power of the minivan's turbo action, when the rest of the family would be asleep, the driver, always one of the boys, would inch the speed up higher and higher to see what the engine was made of. Emeka could personally testify that it did 110 mph like a dream. The van also impressed the muscle cars in the next lane; making eye contact with the driver of a Mustang, the boy would give the van a little power that invited the Mustang driver to open up his own engine, and the two would be on their way, racing at top speeds down the highway. When they happily woke upon arrival at their destination, the rest of the Ihedigbos always wondered why their road trips always seemed so short.

Though the Ihedigbo children did not have much in the way of the gadgets, toys, and accoutrements that are designed to entertain passive, sedentary young people today, they manufactured plenty of fun on their own.

When David, Nate, Emeka, and James hopped on their bikes riding throughout the neighborhood seeking their next adventure, smiling as those without a care in the world, they weaved in and out, up and down the neighborhood streets, jumping curbs, popping wheelies, and waving at their friends who longingly peered out at them, noses pressed against the glass of the front window that looked onto the street. Boys who were their parents' only son grew green with envy at the fact that anytime the Ihedigbo boys were ready to play, they had an instant team of two-on-two basketball, an instant offensive and defensive play line for a football game, or an instant bicycle gang, harmless as they were, but nonetheless a gang of boys who knew, understood, and looked out for one another.

The Ihedigbo bike gang was not without its shenanigans though. As with all groups, there were challenges to be experienced among its members; where there are boys involved, there will be "situations" that incite the emotions and push them to the edge. Every child remembers his first bike and the bike that he loves most. The image of that bike—in most cases, a child's only means of transportation to the pockets of fun around the neighborhood—never leaves the memory, no matter how old we become, and the image of the beloved bike becomes even more heightened when this critical piece of machinery is lost. James experienced one such encounter.

"My mother bought me a brand-new ten-speed bike, the racing-style kind with the elephant handlebars and the skinny tires. Man, I loved that bike! One day, I left the bike outside because I'd planned to go to my friend's house in a little bit. I went into the house to do something, and when I came back, my bike was gone! I was in a panic! I asked my brothers where it was, and my brother Emeka told me that he'd taken my bike and left it at the bus stop and that someone had stolen it! I was so mad at Emeka! In our neighborhood, you walked or rode your bike everywhere, so not having my bike meant that I was stuck!"

The journey to the National Football League (NFL) fame that James enjoys today began when he was only six years old. One day, Rose was driving around town, running one of the many errands that occupy the time of any mother of a large family, when James peered out the window at two groups of little kids dressed in uniforms with large shoulder pads hitting each other. "I said, 'Mom, I want to do that! I want to play *that* game!'" James recalls of the day he was bitten by the football bug. Rose, always one to encourage her children to try new things, discussed the idea with Apollos and then promptly signed her youngest son up to play Pop Warner pee wee football.

"Before then," James explains, "I didn't really play with my brothers because I was too small. After I started playing pee wee ball with my pads, I got more skills and confidence. We would have backyard football games on the weekends where all of the kids in the neighborhood would come to our house and play."

In the backyard of the Ihedigbo home, boys, young and old, would gather to play all out, full-blown tackle football with no pads. "It's where I got my toughness from," James recollects proudly.

David remembers the backyard football games that he and his brothers played with the rest of the boys in the neighborhood fondly. They were surrounded by a number of immigrant families and were always able to coax them into playing at a moment's notice. This was no easy backyard league—not for the faint of heart. It was fast and it was free, but it was rough!

"Our type of play was very rough. There were no pads involved, although we played in fearless competition like we were fully padded, so it was really intense. On that field, we weren't just boys in the neighborhood, we would picture ourselves actually playing in the NFL. You were your favorite player wearing your favorite team's uniform. I was always Ed Reed from the Baltimore Ravens, and James was always Brian Dawkins. We played football for real, with a lot of one-on-one matchups and lots of serious drives."

Emeka also remembers these gridiron games in his family's backyard. "We played violent tackle football like we saw them play on TV—not flag football—with no pads. It's a wonder that none of us got paralyzed or killed!"

As Rose stood inside of her kitchen preparing yam flour for the evening meal, peering out of the curtained window at what seemed like scores of neighborhood boys in her yard, she was all at once concerned and relieved. Her concern came because of the fact that her boys were right outside being hit, pummeled, and pounded as they tried to compete and win the game. There were boys of all sizes out there, big and small, old and young, and she constantly prayed that no one would get seriously hurt. Her relief came as a result of her children finding something to do that they seemed to love so passionately.

The backyard games would start during the daytime and last for hours, the players barely recognizing the fact that the sun had gone down and the streetlights had come on. She would step outside of the door and make the announcement they all knew was inevitable.

"Okay, boys, next touchdown wins the game, and then it's over! It's late…time to come in the house!" she would call out as they would all groan in unison, "Awwww, Mom!"

Pee wee football represented the official beginning of James's love for the game, and this game that the child loved was teaching him some valuable lessons about himself. One of the first observations he made of himself as a player, besides recognizing that he happened to be *really* good at this game, was, "I never wanted to quit the game. I had to show my brothers and the other kids that I was tough enough to play, so I wouldn't let anything stop me, no matter how much it hurt."

While organized football gave James an opportunity for exposure, it was the backyard football league, however, that made him tough. "He took a lot of beatings because he was usually the smallest one on the field," explains his brother David.

After a few years, Emeka, David, and Nate finally allowed little James, who was now nine years old, a spot on the team in their backyard league. In doing so, his brothers soon discovered something incredibly unique about him as they watched him play—something special. Emeka tells the story of this first time he noticed this distinction in his baby brother.

"One day, we were one man down. Almost like clockwork, James said, 'I'll play!' We were big guys, so we said, 'Nah, you're too small, James!' But James insisted. 'Let me play!' he kept saying, so we let him in the game. Right off the bat, he was good. We would throw the ball, and he would catch it, and then someone would tackle him as hard as they could. He was laying there, decimated. Crying. Sobbing. We expected him to get up and go away. Instead, he would get up still sobbing and line up for the next play! We gave him a few moments—still not finished crying. We'd call the snap and hike the ball…and he'd *still* be sobbing! But he was *still good*! We knew this guy was going to be a professional. Those backyard games taught him how to be able to take punishment and dole it out. Now he's one of the hardest-hitting players in the NFL."

In every neighborhood's backyard football league, there is a legendary story—one that every boy in the neighborhood remembers, whether he witnessed it firsthand or not. After all, it is a legend, and it is worthy of telling again and again because of some exceptional feat or accomplishment on the field that defied logic or reason. The legendary story surrounding the Ihedigbo backyard football league just happened to be one of their youngest brother, James Ihedigbo, and it is one best told from eyewitness accounts.

"I'll never forget that day," David explains with eyes shining. "It was a really big play that would determine the game. On one side of our house, there was a wooden fence that came up about waist high. On the other side, there was no fence, so you could run your routes deeper. My brother threw to James a real deep route, and it was like everybody held their breath at the same time because you could see the ball just hanging in the air. James ran into the fence, through the wooden fence, broke the fence, but still caught the ball! Here was this little kid with this huge strength! All everybody could do was gather around him and ask over and over, 'How did you catch that *ball*? How could you have *caught* that ball?' It was amazing. James had fence marks all over his chest, and you could tell he was in a lot of pain, but we won.

James never complained, he didn't have anything to say except, 'We won the game!' This was competition at its best and showed that James would do whatever it took to get to the next level and shine. That is a quality that has never left him from high school all the way through to the NFL."

🍃

Apollos was dedicated not only to taking care of his own family but others back in Nigeria, for it was out of 29 Tamarack Drive that Rose and Apollos began to launch their plans for the Nigerian-American Technological and Agricultural College (NATAC). Their return to Nigeria had always been a part of the plan; they were simply waiting for God's season to turn this dream into a reality. The Ihedigbo children describe their father as "obsessed" about going back to Nigeria and giving back to his people.

Even before they began the school in their homeland, Apollos would make plans to periodically return to his home village with many of the things that his relatives back home needed. Over many months, he would collect clothing of all sizes to take back with him on the long plane ride to Nigeria. With each visit to the Survival Center, he would bring back additional pants, shirts, dresses, and shoes for his imminent return to Africa where he would shower the much-needed clothing on those who awaited his return.

As a result, the house was always cluttered, so much so that the children would refrain from inviting their friends over to hang out. If their friends would dare enter the home, they would encounter an unusual sight: tons of suitcases everywhere, from the bedroom to the living room where they were piled so high in the corner that they reached the ceiling! Furthermore, there were endless boxes of clothing throughout the house that would soon be packed away in the suitcases in preparation for Apollos's travel back to the village, which always seemed just around the corner.

Once the Ihedigbo children grew up, they often wondered, thinking back on all of the additional suitcases their father would carry with him back to the village, how their parents afforded all of this excess luggage they brought along. When they had the mind to ask about the extra fees, their father simply explained, "We just saved up the money to bring the bags along. The Lord provided."

Indeed the Lord did provide—and over and over again at that—for each and every one of these bags would eventually make their way to bless hundreds of lives, all thanks to the man who was determined to take care of everyone, Apollos Ihedigbo.

ANOTHER KIND OF DIFFERENT: THE IMPOSSIBILITY OF BLENDING IN

The sometimes harsh and uncomfortable realities of being an "other" in society made the need for fellowship among their own cultural group a necessity—necessary for social, emotional, and mental health. The sense of acceptance and belonging that the Nigerian community offered in the midst of a larger society that was not always so accepting made it that much more valuable.

Apollos and Rose knew how necessary it was to keep their children connected to their roots, especially since their offspring lived most of their lives in a school context that silently demanded their conformity in order to be accepted. Hence, Nigerian gatherings were a must, as they provided a sense of culture and connection that it was impossible for the children to otherwise receive in the suburbs.

The children themselves looked forward to these gatherings as well, as they were great fun. James recalls some of his fondest memories in heading to these Nigerian affairs. "We always looked forward to it," he remembers with a smile. "It was a great time with great food, and lots of aunties, uncles, cousins, and music. They were so festive, and it felt good because we got to see people that we didn't get to see on a regular basis. It was like being around hundreds of family members, and it was no different from a family reunion. Times like these provided me with something that I didn't get from the culture on the Amherst front—a sense of acceptance and connectedness."

Just by virtue of enjoying an American education, the children of an immigrant family will be exposed to various values and practices that fall outside of what is traditionally accepted in their un-Westernized homes.

"We were a very tight family with very strict parents and very strong biblical beliefs," Nate explains of his early childhood. "The kids at school and the American kids who lived in the apartment complex were just…different. They introduced us to things that we did not know about, we were just seeing kids act like this for the first time because we didn't act that way as Nigerians," he recalls. "For example, when I was in the first grade, the neighborhood boys got their hands on a Polaroid camera, which my brothers and I had never seen before, and they started doing dumb stuff like taking pictures of their butts and doing other nasty stuff with the camera. We were mortified just witnessing that kind of behavior. We would have *never* thought of doing things like that!"

Further, the Ihedigbo children could easily be marked as "others" when it came to the way they treated their elders and how their level of respect for those older than they were differed from that of their classmates. In the home, they respected their parents greatly, politely relating to them, paying deference to them, and recognizing that they were the leaders and authoritarians of the household. Simply put, Mom and Dad were in charge. Their neighborhood friends on the other hand, especially the white ones, would not hesitate to talk back disrespectfully to their parents, rebel against their instructions, and throw fits when they did not get their way. In those households, the boys observed, it was unclear who was in charge!

Emeka, Nate, David, and James would marvel when they witness such things as this at the homes of their neighborhood friends. As young as they were, it seemed to them that those households lacked something very important, though they could not put their finger on it at the time. Observing the dramatic difference of what they experienced at home versus their friends' houses, they decided that the missing elements were fear and accountability.

Here, there was no fear of consequences and no accountability. The American kids that surrounded them knew that if their mother or father got out of line, all the kid would have to do was pick up the phone and call the Department of Child Protective Services and Mom and Dad would have to suffer the consequences. As a result, instead of the kids having a fear of the parents, the parents had a fear of their children, which led them on most occasions to acquiesce to the child's demands. The same lack of fear, respect, and reverence for consequences led to their friends acting irreverently throughout the neighborhood and at school.

As James and David made a visit to the mall, for example, they witnessed a young white child yelling at his mother in the store as he held up an expensive pair of basketball shoes.

"I want *this* pair of shoes, Mom! I *swear*, Mom, why are you so *dumb*? Why don't you listen to me and get me what I *want*?" the child yelled loudly. Embarrassed and humiliated, the red-faced mother tried to soothe and calm her "spirited" child down.

The brothers looked at one another in amazement, each ensuring that the other had just witnessed what would have gotten them knocked out in their own culture.

"Did you *see* that?" James asked with a smile of disbelief.

To this, David answered, "Yes! I wish I *would* try to swear at my mom! It would be the first *and* the very last time!" They both laughed, knowing it was true. Such behavior would never be tolerated in their community. It was here that they marked another cultural difference: Nigerian children understood what it took for their parents to get where they were, so they valued whatever their parents could afford for them.

The American model of family that surrounded them seemed so off kilter to the Ihedigbo boys! In their own home, as well as in the homes of their Nigerian cousins, the situation was quite the opposite.

David explains, "In America, the family system seems to have been thrown out of the window. There were times when I was growing up when I was scared of not only getting a beating from my mom but my uncle and aunt. Any uncle or aunt who saw me do something wrong had the power to put me back in line. They don't have that in American culture. If a kid gets out of line and is punished, he will call the authorities. There is *no way* that would happen in a Nigerian family. The moms and dads would never let it happen!"

David goes on to describe the process of the "It Takes a Village to Raise a Child" discipline that is characteristic of the Nigerian community. "At Nigerian functions, I've seen kids act up and get slapped by someone *else's* parents. 'What are you doing?' they would ask the kid. Then the kid would not talk back. Instead, he would just say, 'I'm sorry. I shouldn't have been doing that.' But that's not the end of it. The kid would go and tell his own parents what happened and why he got slapped so that he wouldn't get into even more trouble when the report got back to his mom and dad. They would discipline him for what he had done too, saying, 'You've been taught better than that. Why would you do such a thing?' In Nigerian culture, you learned from your mistakes, you were not resentful about the discipline, and you definitely didn't even think about calling child services. We understood that if you did not act up, you would not get reprimanded. Everything was cause and effect."

Additionally, the Ihedigbos extended this respect for their elders outside of their household, as their parents had trained them to do. While their friends, again the mainstream white ones, would not hesitate to call an adult by his or her first name, the Ihedigbo children were accustomed to calling adults within their community uncle or auntie. They would be mortified to ever attempt to call a Nigerian adult, or any adult for that matter, by a first name.

Another clear differentiation between the Ihedigbos and their American counterparts was one that the children picked up on almost immediately: the spirit of entitlement. For some reason, they observed, their neighborhood and school friends felt that others owed them something—a second chance, an easier option, an extension of a deadline, the right to enjoy a certain privilege without putting in the work, the acceptance of an excuse, a free pass, or whatever it is they were demanding at the time.

The Ihedigbos, on the other hand, had been trained up all their lives with a different mentality: no one owes you anything, so whatever you want, you must work hard to obtain yourself. They were grateful that their parents had engrained this way of thinking into their young minds and wondered how long their American counterparts would go in life before they understood that the world did not owe them a thing.

Because he was a natural athlete, James did not limit himself to playing football; he also ventured out to play lacrosse. However, his high school lacrosse career was short-lived. "The kids who played lacrosse were kind of preppy, suburban, all-American players. Though I grew up in the suburbs as well, their attitude of self-righteousness, self-importance, and overprivilege turned me off. I wasn't raised that way, so although I was cool with them, I didn't fit in, so I quit the team."

Being an African in Massachusetts is like being a black panther walking in the snow; blending into such surroundings is no easy feat. Such was the case for the Ihedigbo children who had to navigate a context that is challenging enough for even the most "typical" of American child. Negotiating the rules of friendship, boyfriends and girlfriends, making good grades, what to wear, where to sit in the lunchroom, keeping up with the cool kids, and staying out harm's way by avoiding the bullies are difficult enough without having to face the challenge of being the most obvious outsider of the entire group.

As Africans, the Ihedigbo children were used to being different. Nowhere was this notion truer than in the way they dressed. Their clothing was different. They did not wear the flashy name-brand clothing that set the class boundaries of cool, popular, and unpopular within the trendy, upscale Massachusetts schools they attended. The kids at school wore brands like Polo, Izod, and Liz Claiborne; however, the Ihedigbo kids wore "clothes," just clothes. While the kids at school wore Nike and Puma sneakers, the Ihedigbos wore "shoes," just shoes—Survival Center shoes.

The differences in external appearance that marked this unique Nigerian family also showed forth in their cultural expressions, particularly Rose's way of ethnically styling Onyii's hair. Not everyone in Onyii's non-diverse school was fond of Rose's painstakingly elaborate techniques of fashioning her daughter's hair and sending her into a sea of curious, merciless white kindergarteners at Marks Meadow Elementary School.

"One time," Onyii explains, "my mom spent the whole night putting my hair in plaits—the kind that are wrapped really tight with thread and that stick out so you can shape and mold them any way you want. Because they were tight, my head hurt *so* badly. 'What is that on your hair? Why does your hair look like that?' all the kids would ask as they reached out to touch it, mocking me. I was really embarrassed and went crying to my teacher to ask her if I could take the plaits out. She and I took them out together, and when I got home, my mom was soooo mad! She kept asking, 'Why would you take them out, Onyii? Why would you *do* that?'"

"It really broke my heart to hear that the other kids were teasing my child because they did not understand her hair," Rose explains, reflecting on the ordeal with a shake of the head. "Onyii was traumatized and bullied by her classmates who repeatedly called her names and made her cry over her hair. I was shocked that the teacher let this go on so many times! I went to the teacher time after time to meet with her—just about my daughter's *hair*! Each time I went, I demanded that the teacher do something about the problem, and each time, she would say that she would talk with the students, though nothing ever really changed."

Sometimes our pain is so real, so palpable, and so utterly inconceivable in life that we maintain some remnant or keepsake of it to remind ourselves in the future about the magnitude of the heartbreaking experiences we have overcome. The reason for our saving these mementos varies as widely as the broad spectrum of experiences that we encounter. Perhaps we keep them as evidence of pain that was so agonizing that without such evidence, those to whom we tell the story would never believe it happened. Perhaps we hold on to them in anticipation of the opportunity to reflect upon them later in life and celebrate ourselves for our diligence and determination to overcome life's obstacles. Perhaps we hold on to them to test the diminishing emotional impact that the experiences related to these tokens have on our lives over the years. Regardless of why we guard them so closely, these mementos matter to us and fill a need that only we ourselves can define. Such is the case in a letter written to Onyii (Debbie) by one of her elementary school classmates kept in a safe place by her mother, Rose. Reading the letter today still elicits raw emotion in the heart of a protective mother who saw the very image of her proud Nigerian self reflected in her daughter.

Debbie,

My friends don't like your kind! Beacaus [sic] you don't have any nice clowhs [sic]. And your [sic] in 3rd grade and, my friends and I are all in 4th! And your [sic] not my kind! And I know much more than you and if you tell on me that will just pruve [sic] that you're a baby, and it will just mack [sic] things whours [sic]. So if you just shut your mouth nouthing will happen [sic]. But if you tell, I will kill you!!–Karen X. P.S. DON'T Tell!!!!!!

"Things did not change until we left that school and went to a different one when Onyii was in fourth grade," Rose recalls. "To this day, I do not know why those students did not understand her or her hair and why they bullied her for it."

The move of their daughter from Marks Meadow Elementary School to Fort River Elementary School resulted in a much better environment for young Onyii. While some might have viewed the change as giving in to the hostile Western society that surrounded them, for Rose it was quite the opposite. The change was for her daughter's safety, but she never felt the pressure to change her daughter's Nigerian hairstyles.

"I insisted on helping my daughter understand why she was wearing her hair this way, and I taught her to ignore the bullies that did not understand why she wore her hair this way," Rose reveals proudly. "I never felt the pressure to conform to what they were doing contrary to my African culture. As a result, Onyii continued to grow and mature, she learned how to avoid the bullies, and she became stronger in defending herself!" For Rose, a Nigerian in America, there would be no compromise—no defeat.

Though not as dramatic, the Ihedigbo boys had their own challenges in making their way through a very white, very unexposed school system. "I remember being in elementary school where the kids called me African booty scratcher," Emeka explains. "Then one day, I was just sitting there at my desk, and a little white girl came up to me and said, 'Hey, can I touch your hair?' I said no, but she reached out and started rubbing it anyway. She turned to her friends and said, 'It feels like a rug!' I felt more like a specimen than a human being. They were so culturally different, and the transition was tough."

Fortunately, by the time he'd entered high school, James, the youngest of the Ihedigbo clan, had an advantage. James had seen his four older siblings take on the assimilation battles of being "the African in the school," a fact that automatically made them different than the school's population norm. However, James had another advantage working in his favor: he was quite successful at sports, so students wanted to be around him.

"People wanted to be around me and to be my friend because being good at sports made me one of the cool kids. Because I was an athlete, people just accepted me for who I was, regardless of where my family was from, and I accepted them as well," he explains.

It was not only that which was seen on the exterior that differentiated the Nigerian children from their American counterparts; it was the unique way they smelled.

Onyii recalls, "When I was seven or eight years old, kids used to whisper and say that I and my brothers smelled. I would ask, 'What do you mean?' We never noticed a smell. The kids would say, 'You don't wear deodorant!' and we didn't, so there was nothing I could say to that. But I didn't know that we *smelled bad* until they told me. To us, we just smelled like Nigerians. Nigerians have always had a natural smell."

Even though the "Nigerian smell" was not an issue for the Ihedigbos, it was clearly an issue for their non-Nigerian guests.

"We always had a fear of people coming over to our house because they were not used to our smell. When I was in junior high, my friend Susie came over to the house, and after that one time, she never wanted to come back to our house again. She said our house smelled different. After that day, I became supersensitive to smell. Today, I smell things all the time, and if I smell anything in my house, I do not want people to come over. I instantly want odors eliminated as soon as I smell them. It's so bad now that my husband thinks I have a disorder!"

After being enlightened on the impact that she and her brothers' malodorous state was having on their social standing among the other kids in school, this made some—though not all of the children—want to wear deodorant. However, the request to wear deodorant could easily be mistaken as one's desire to be less Nigerian and more American, and knowing this, Onyii broached the topic delicately with her father. It wasn't as much of a challenge as she thought it would be.

"I was standing around with my dad in the health and beauty section of K-Mart one day, and I decided to ask, 'Dad, why don't we wear deodorant?' My dad simply shrugged and said, 'I don't know.' I asked, 'Can I get some?' He said, 'Sure.' And that was that. I picked up a pretty pink and white bottle of Suave deodorant that day and never looked back."

Onyii, the eldest, was accustomed to being the trendsetter in the family. In the same way that she was first to adopt the American standard of using deodorant, she was also the first to incorporate the use of shampoo in her beauty regimen.

"We always used to use bar soap on our hair. I remember seeing a shampoo commercial once and asked my mom why we didn't use shampoo. Her reply was, 'It's all the same thing. Shampoo is the same as Irish Spring!' After I insisted, we got shampoo and were using it by the time I got to high school."

The ways of life that made the Ihedigbos different from those around them did not always occur behind the four walls of a local Nigerian home. In fact, anyone watching the family closely would catch nuances of behaviors that were telltale signs that this family was a bit different than the typical Massachusetts family. One such incident occurred when the children's maternal grandmother herself, Helen, traveled to Massachusetts from Nigeria for a visit. Grandmother knew that she was different—she openly acknowledged it—but this did not bother her, for she simply did not care. As with any older person, she knew exactly who she was and what she wanted to do and no one would stop her.

The family station wagon rolled slowly up to the First Baptist Church in Amherst. The children, faces shiny and clothes neatly pressed, filed out of the car in an orderly fashion in the parking lot, their shiny hand-me-down shoes reflecting the light of the warm summer sun. Rose proudly looked her children over, as was her custom every Sunday morning, to ensure that all gently worn shirts were tucked, all pants were securely belted, all faces were shiny and clean.

As was the children's custom every Sunday morning, they walked in a calm and orderly fashion towards the door of the church, eager to see their friends. On this particular Sunday, Grandmother Helen was a part of the processional into the church. As they made their way from the car to the church door, Rose proudly introduced her mother to her other friends who were also arriving in the parking lot.

"Please meet my mother. Mother, meet my friends." The introductions continued as the children stood around and greeted their own friends.

In a moment, however, things changed as the children saw something that stopped them dead in their tracks. In the middle of a parking-lot introduction to one of Rose's fellow church members, Grandmother, who wore a *wrappa* (a large, colorful piece of African cloth wrapped around the body and tucked in at the waist), spread her legs apart and relieved herself on the ground—in a very deliberate, conspicuous fashion! What their grandmother had done was impossible to not notice, and her grandchildren Nate, James, Emeka, David, and Onyii were eye-witnesses—horrified ones! They'd heard the sound of the water hitting the cool paved asphalt before they saw it, and then they turned to watch in utter amazement as their grandmother peed on the ground right next to a car—standing straight up and without concern or fear of any critique of onlookers!

"Oh no! Grandmother's peeing in the parking lot!" they whispered with guarded embarrassment, shock, and horror as they nudged one another in disbelief.

"Grandmother, what did you *do*?" Nate questioned as he turned towards his family's matriarch, eyes wide as saucers at what he'd just witnessed and hoping none outside the family had seen such a thing.

"I relieved myself," she answered nonchalantly. "I had to relieve myself, so I relieved myself," she explained unapologetically. With that, she proudly lifted her head and proceeded to walk in stately fashion through the front doors of the church and into worship leaving her little puddle behind!

Sometimes it was the Ihedigbos themselves that marked the fact that they were different from their surroundings, and other times, as in the case of Grandma's visit to church, it was others. Another such case is a story that the family recalls with laughter about Uncle Smarts, an uncle that lived with the family while they lived in the university apartments at UMass.

There was clearly a commotion going on outside of the apartment window. An uncharacteristic amount of loud voices and laughter summonsed several of the Ihedigbos out of their rest and into the bright, warm outdoors. As they stepped outside, they caught sight of a man moving as fast as a cheetah, running through the grassy courtyard in an all-out sprint.

"Eh! Eh! Eh!" he called out excitedly to his family that now stood by as he tried to run and point at the same time towards thick, brushy squirrels running for their dear lives. "Good meats! Good meats! Eh! Good meats!"

"Oh no! What is he *doing*?" one of the Ihedigbo boys asked, expressing the shared horror and embarrassment of his siblings.

The squirrels darted up the first trees they could find, sensing that their predator meant business. All around, people laughed at Uncle Smarts who chased after the innocent creatures in pursuit of "good meats." While they laughed, the Ihedigbo youngsters could only shake their heads and return into their apartment where they were safe from ridicule and sheltered from being so different. In fact, in a self-protective effort, they began to refer to their Uncle Smarts as Uncle Dumb so that others would not associate them with their uncle—and that they would not think that the Ihedigbos ate squirrel.

Of course, squirrel was not on the menu at the Ihedigbo house; however, the foods they ate were different from that which sat on the tables of the homes surrounding them. Early on when the kids were younger, their mother cooked up an abundance of Nigerian food like palm oil, *egusi* soup, stews, rice, yams, and traditional West African fare, only occasionally tossing in American delicacies like spaghetti and hot dogs for the children.

As they grew older, and especially as the kids learned to cook for themselves, the menu migrated towards more American cuisine like chicken wings, hamburgers, and the like. Though all of the siblings learned to cook, Onyii was the first to learn, and Rose trained her children well in making the Nigerian staples.

However, when their mother and father were away and Onyii had to cook dinner for her brothers, their assimilated tastes demanded selections from the American side of the menu, and she complied.

Even today when the family gets together, instead of going to a restaurant, someone will run to the store to pick up some ingredients, and together they will prepare a feast in the kitchen. While Emeka is the professional in the restaurant industry and loves preparing his unusual chef selections, each Ihedigbo has his or her specialty: James makes chicken wings, David makes lasagna, Nate makes rice and stew, and Onyii makes macaroni and cheese.

Other differentiating elements, like the difficulty of writing the last name "Ihedigbo," an exercise which often caused the children to run late or miss out on recess because they had not finished writing their names like their shorter and simpler-surnamed counterparts, helped to set the Ihedigbos apart as the "others" in the community. While they could do nothing about their last name, by the time Onyii and Emeka reached high school, they decided to go by their more American middles names of "Debbie" (for Deborah) and "Joseph" respectively. These names were much more culturally friendly in the city of Amherst. They would not pick up their Igbo names again until after they had graduated from high school.

The Ihedigbo kids further understood the extent of their differences when their neighborhood friends would ask, "What did your mom and dad just say?" Not meaning any slight to Rose and Apollos, their friends found it difficult to understand their parents' thick Nigerian accents when they came over the Ihedigbo house for a visit. It could not be mistaken that the Ihedigbos were special in so many ways.

VALUES, SPIRITUALITY AND SUCCESS: THE IHEDIGBO STANDARD

If you walked into the Ihedigbo household on any given afternoon, regardless of the evening or the occasion, the scene would be the same: the dedicated mother would take her place in the kitchen to prepare dinner for the family. The siblings would be dispersed throughout the house playing video games, reading a book, or watching television. You would witness children relaxing peacefully, unfazed by the worries and concerns of the world around them that worried themselves into anxiety with their desires of having it all.

The Ihedigbos realized that they indeed had it all as long as they had one another, and their gathering place was this sofa—this comfortable, cozy, sleep-inducing sofa that served as the central meeting place for family meetings, discussions about legacy, the dispensation of age-old advice from the parents, and an escape from the world around them that called them different.

The Ihedigbo progeny were not your typical sibling matchups filled with bitter contest and bickering. Though there were typical brotherly disputes, the children had been reared in an environment of love and were taught to demonstrate love and respect towards one another at all times.

Onyii, valuing the relationship that she had with her younger brother, and all of her brothers for that matter, would saunter over to the sofa and lay her head on the strong shoulder of one of several men who would lay down their lives to protect her. Not only was there love among the youngsters who shared a common struggle to fit into a society in which they were clear and evident standouts, there was a sense of respect and dignity that they challenged one another to uphold, often without even saying a word. They were Ihedigbos.

Guests to the home would often be awestruck by the love and affection that the children of the clan openly displayed towards one another. It was so unusual, the uninhibitedly affectionate and tender relationship that these children shared among themselves. It so beautiful, that it was strange. Not strange in the sense that there was something oddly wrong with the way they related to each other, but strange in the sense that it seemed so, so typically un-American!

Par for the course in most American households is a display of kids running around, kicking, screaming, fighting, trying to get the advantage over brothers and sisters, whether younger or older, in an effort to rule the household. However, the Ihedigbos were different, as most guests observed jealously, especially those who had combative, bickering children of their own who tortured each other nonstop.

A casual observer could not help but wonder after observing the five Ihedigbo children in action what their parents could have possibly done to raise such loving children who nurtured bonds of love instead of grudges with one another.

"How could they have possibly gotten these children to peacefully coexist?" they would wonder to themselves as they stared intently at the youngsters, secretly trying to derive tips and lessons of their own to use in dealing with their own children. "If only I could get *my* kids to act like this towards one another, my life would be *so* much easier!" they would think.

Ask any Ihedigbo-surnamed child who grew up under the roof of two doctors of education what the two most important values promoted by their parents were, and they will consistently, unanimously give the pollster the same two answers without a second thought: a relationship with God and education. At every opportunity, Apollos and Rose instilled these values, utilizing every possible teaching moment as an opportunity to do just that—teach or disseminate values.

When they were at the dinner table, values: God has been good to you, and after you finish dinner, go study for your exam. When they were watching a television show, values: live your life as a good witness for Christ, and be an example to the rest of your class by making good grades. When the family members were out collecting cans together on Saturday mornings for extra money, values: the Lord will provide. Get a good education so that you can have a better life. When the kids got caught up in day-to-day sibling conflict, values: learn to love and forgive one another like Christ loves you as a way of life, and when you go away to college one day, you will realize how much you need one another.

The parental influence of Apollos and Rose did not only permeate the household, but it followed the children everywhere they went. There was something about their childrearing that in some ways insulated their children from adopting certain attitudes that fueled the thoughts and actions of youth around them, namely the attitude of "There are certain things I cannot do, Mom and Dad, because I've got to be cool."

Mind you, no youth is immune to the need to fit in among his peers by participating in or abstaining from certain behaviors that are considered taboo for his age group. But the Ihedigbos were different: they discovered a unique way to fit into the youth culture around them without compromising the values and beliefs of their parents, values and beliefs that were instilled and nurtured through generation after generation in their Nigerian villages. Values that said hard work pays off. Where there's a will, there's a way. Respect your elders, and treat one another with high consideration, that is, every man, no matter how different he is than you. Values that said to love and take care of your family members, and above all, honor your parents and treat them with the utmost of respect. Values that taught that God will always provide, and that if you trust Him with your life and meditate on His word, you will have good success.

Emeka recalls, "My father's words were almost prophetic. He would say things like, 'Tomorrow, I'm not going to be here and you need to be able to carry yourself as an Ihedigbo. You must use these values to be strong and intelligent and to have success—but not the success that you think is befitting for you. You must be attuned to the path the Lord has laid out for you, only in there will you have success and all the desires of your heart will come to pass.' He said it so much that it almost became too redundant. After hearing it over and over for years and years, you wanted to say, 'Dad, okay! We got it! Can you give it a rest?' He never did. Today, I know he was 100 percent right."

The strong values that had been deeply ingrained into these children from the moment of their birth behind the four walls of whatever abode the Ihedigbos called home was evident to the outside world. As soon as they stepped out of the old station wagon or minivan—for practicality, they would always have a family-sized car, for this family was great in number—they were well behaved and organized.

Crossing the parking lot to go into church, they proceeded respectfully and orderly, dressed in perfectly starched and neatly pressed hand-me-downs from other people's closets that comprised their wardrobes. They entered this sacred place with reverence week in and week out, this place that would reaffirm their values in a God that knew all about them and that kept them day by day. A relationship with God was not just for the Apollos and Rose, but for Onyii, David, Emeka, Nate, and James. Unlike with the close-knit home they all shared, when it came to a relationship with God, each one had to have his or her own.

A family friend reflects, "There they would be in church, all lined up in their neat, colorful outfits on one of the front pews where they always sat because Apollos was a deacon. The pastor would be preaching, and Rose would stand up and shout 'Amen!' while Apollos would say 'Amen!' from his seat as he smiled and nodded approvingly, but they were not alone. I was amazed to see their children actually paying attention—actually singing along when the church sang a song or psalm. Seeing this family who had come to this country and maintained such a spirit of strength in the midst of everything they struggled through, bringing their family up in the Lord—it was something that made you stand up and take notice. It wasn't forced or fake. You could see it was real, not just with Apollos and Rose, but with all of them. Such a level of commitment and dignity. To see these same values that brought the Ihedigbos here flowing into their children was just a completely awesome thing to see, especially in a world where children are dragged to church and pretty much just endure the service until it is over."

Onyii, Emeka, David, Nate and James could not help but absorb some degree of spirituality by living under the roof of Apollos and Rose Ihedigbo. Not only did they teach their children to have faith in God through leading by silent example, knowing all eyes were on them and that their response to any challenge or crisis would forever shape their children's ability to believe in God's faithfulness one way or the other, but their words to their children were full of faith.

"Mom was always so spiritually in tune to everything," James explains. Everything was 'Pray about it,' 'Pray over it,' or 'By

God's faith.' Every time there was an issue, Mom's answer was always 'By the will of God' and 'You've got to place it in God's hands,' and she would always say, 'I would not be where I am without the grace of God over my life and my children.'" Rose was adamant about being a spiritual example for her children, and her words and active-believer's lifestyle greatly influenced the hearts and minds of her children.

James goes on to explain, "My mom and I have this thing that we've been doing since I was in high school. Before every game, I will call her and we'll pray together. In high school and college, we would pray before I walked out on the field. In the NFL, we pray before I leave for the stadium. We have prayed before every game I've played in the NFL. She prays for protection over me, for victory, and that God would see His glory through my play and what He has blessed me with. I lift him up any opportunity I get. I have been blessed to play this game, so I never take the credit for it. I always say, 'It's not me, it's God.' I couldn't do what I do on the football field without His hand on me."

Prayer and devotion were a strong part of the family's daily life. Apollos and Rose were always calling on God alone as a couple and with their entire family.

"Whenever there was a need, my mom would say that we were putting everything in God's hands. She would always also say that a prayer with no action is a dead prayer. You have to put in action and effort," David explains. "That is why after they would pray for provision, many times they would wake us up on Saturday morning, take us out to where college students had been partying the night before, and we would all collect cans to get money for food," he remembers. "That's also the reason why my dad would work three jobs to put food on the table. Later on, my mom would drive more than eighty miles a day to and from her job to make ends meet. You can pray, but you've got to put some action behind it!"

More than lecture their children on prayer, the Apollos and Rose lived it out before them. When the kids would wake up on Saturday morning, they were accustomed to their mother making them a nice big hot breakfast: pancakes, French toast, eggs, and all. However, before breakfast, it was customary for their parents' door to be closed right before breakfast time as Rose and Apollos prayed in their room together. The children always knew that their parents were praying behind those closed doors—they could hear them—and they waited patiently for their breakfast, knowing it was just on the other side of prayer. After breakfast, Apollos would lead the family in a special time of devotion. The kids enjoyed these special family times and found them to be quite fun.

As strong academicians themselves, nothing in the way of their children's academics escaped their sight. James, who the family recognized to be a naturally-gifted athlete, did not receive any passes on his classroom duties as a result of his superstardom on the hardwood or the football field. No child, no matter how talented, how decorated, or how popular at school, was exempt.

"After basketball practice," he explains, "I would come home and do my homework, and then my dad would tell me to bring it to him so he could see it, and then he would quiz me on it. I would get so frustrated because this was the last thing I wanted to do, but he would say to me, 'You don't know it until you can teach it. You're not going to just play basketball and forget about your school work.'" Thus, the elder Ihedigbo held his children highly accountable to be as equally accomplished in their academic pursuits as in their athletic pursuits.

"He wanted us to be in athletics because he knew the fundamental disciplines that came with it like teamwork and good character," explains James. "He'd even played soccer himself back in Nigeria, not professionally, but for fun. However, my dad knew that ultimate success came from education. That was how he built his success, and that was how he wanted us to build ours. 'You can't be the best in sports unless you are the best in education as well,' is what he would say."

Like James, David was naturally talented in sports and had a special affinity that had anything to do with athletics. He had played Pop Warner little league football for as long as he could remember and loved to be surrounded by athletes. Whether he himself was playing was unimportant; as long as he was participating in some fashion—managing, training, or cheering on the players from the sidelines, sports were David's comfort zone. He saw himself going far in football, this game that he loved, but he knew that in order to be a success at it, he would have to put in the hard work and effort. David's love for football indeed took him far, having a significant influence on the major he would eventually choose in college: sports management.

When it came to education in the Ihedigbo household, neither Apollos nor Rose pressed it as an option. Instead, they led by example, allowing each of their children to see how hard they worked, dedicating themselves to their studies and not allowing any challenges to get in the way of pursuing their educational goals. Further, they constantly reinforced to their children that this education was not to just build a better life for Mom and Dad, and not even for their family, but for the country of Nigeria.

Sitting around the dinner table, they would constantly explain to young Onyii, Emeka, Nate, David, and James how they were going to take their knowledge and resources back to share them with those in Nigeria who were not as advantaged as they were to come to the U.S. and study. The children saw this model and heard this plan discussed almost every day of their lives in the Ihedigbo household; thus, for them to not value education as highly or to use what they have learned to serve others would be next to impossible.

If one of their youth came home with a negative mark on a report card, the issue never went unaddressed. Apollos would sit down with them and counsel them from a godly perspective. "These are the principles we live by," he would instruct. "These are the things you and I believe are true. These are the things we consider to be important. As a result, this the way you should act," he would say.

Whatever it took to help her children fulfill their educational dreams, Rose would do. Especially after her beloved Apollos passed away, Rose knew that it was up to her to get each one of her kids through university, and she would do so no matter what the sacrifice.

"Whenever I saw them struggling, I reminded them that there was no option of skipping their education or dropping out. It was not an option. 'You have to finish up!' I would say, and I meant it!" Rose explains.

Apollos taught values as a lifestyle. On many occasions, there were situations in which he'd made a significant deposit in the lives of his offspring that they would not recognize for years to come—even years after their father's passing away. The moment of such recognition would be bittersweet, as the child would realize how much further ahead they could be if only they would have valued the deposit at the moment it was made.

David had a bittersweet moment like this of his own. "My dad was a very wise man. It wasn't until he passed away that I sat down and thought about some of the things he'd said. There was one lesson my dad would try to teach me every single day: 'When the sun rises and the sun sets, you can never get that day again.' Whenever he would say this, I would say to myself, *What is this guy talking about?* As a result, I simply thought, *So what? I can do whatever I want to do tomorrow if I don't get it done today.* However, later on in life when I took time to think about it, it really hit me. If you haven't done everything possible to the best of your ability to advance, progress, and make yourself better, you just put yourself one step behind. If you can say that you did do these things, you will always be better than you were yesterday and you will be the person you need to be when you step into tomorrow. Reflecting on this lesson he taught me so many years ago is what keeps me going today, making me want to excel, achieve, and make every day better than the last."

Onyii would also later reflect on how her father ingrained values into her as a lifestyle. Apollos had always dreamt of his daughter, Onyii, becoming engaged to a man that was very spiritual, strong in the Word of God through the traditional Nigerian process—a wine ceremony in which the couple asked for permission in marriage. However, choosing a more Westernized model of courtship and engagement, Austin-born information technology professional Humphrey Brown III and Onyii got engaged, chose a convenient date for the wedding, and announced it to everyone.

Because Apollos was in Nigeria establishing his college at the time, making it difficult to reach him by phone, Rose communicated the news to him that his eldest child had gotten engaged. Clearly upset and put off by the lack of formality and their rejection of the Nigerian engagement process, Apollos made his sentiments clear to Onyii in a neatly handwritten letter.

"My dad wrote me the most amazing letter from Nigeria about how much he wanted me to be happy with Humphrey and that he loved me so much. I cried many tears as I read it, especially as he said, 'You are the apple of my eye' in Igbo. He would say this to me all the time. The letter also said that he was going to fly back to the States from Nigeria to walk me down the aisle. I was so relieved and thankful to God for a dad that loved me so much and wanted me to be happy, despite the fact that we didn't do things his way."

Apollos and Onyii shared a very special relationship in the Spirit. Throughout her life, Apollos not only demonstrated his faith to his eldest child and only daughter, but he taught her to seek God for herself and rely on Him for all of her needs, including provision. A key lesson in this spiritual principle came during this same season of planning Onyii's wedding to her husband, Humphrey Brown III.

"A week before the wedding, we realized that we didn't have enough money, so I called my dad and asked, 'What should we do?'"

"Onyii, where was Jesus's first miracle?" he asked his daughter whom he loved.

"At a wedding," she replied, remembering the many times she'd heard him teach the story.

To this, her father simply replied, "God always provides, Onyii."

This was not an unusual exchange between Onyii and her father who always sought to help his children find their own answers according to the things of God rather than feeding the answers to them directly.

"*That's* how I learned the word of God," Onyii explains. "He always, *always*, referred to the Word of God when I had a situation. Whenever I would ask him a question, he would ask me a question right back. 'What happened when the children did this?' he would ask. 'What did Jesus say to Peter?' He never gave me the answer. I would run to the Word to find out. My dad sent me to the Word because he was such a man of faith," she proudly reflects of her father.

"Though he'd always given me money before, he didn't give me the money this time. He simply said that God would provide, and true to His Word, God did provide: the wedding went off just fine. My dad walked me down the aisle, he went back to Massachusetts, he flew back to Nigeria, and then he passed away."

IGBOS IN THE HOUSE: MAINTAINING THE CULTURAL CONNECTION IN AMERICA

"Cha, cha, cha! Igbo kwenu!" Apollos would call out loudly to the Nigerian crowd in his thick Nigerian accent. "Are the Igbos in the house?"

"Yeah! Yeah!" the crowd would reply back with enthusiasm in undeniably strong immigrant accents, excited about this traditional call and response ritual that marked the formal beginning of their meeting.

"Cha, cha, cha! Nigeria kwenu!" the elder Ihedigbo would call out again to the crowd. "Are the Nigerians in the house?"

"Yeah! Yeah!" the Nigerians would reply, comforted by the close presence of one another as they squeezed four and five to a sofa and two or three to a chair with their African brothers and sisters anticipating what new and interesting intelligence they would learn about their homeland.

At this point, as one of the eldest and most respected Igbo present at the gathering, Apollos would officiate over the ceremonial rituals of the meeting. First, there was the breaking of bread in which he would present, then bless, then break the kola nut, an especially bitter nut resembling what most Americans would consider to look like a root and was always featured at Igbo traditional rituals and ceremonies. As the elder, he would eat of the kola nut first by taking a piece of it from the dish that was placed before him by the homeowner or host—a dish dedicated in the home specifically for the presentation of the sacred kola nut—and then share it by passing it around the room, spreading it around from left to right for the rest of the Nigerians to partake of it.

Eventually, the kola nut from which every family had shared—excluding the children—would come back to the elder, and he would then pass additional items to be shared: pepper seed and peanut butter, which was passed around on a plate and which each family member would scrape onto their piece of kola nut before eating. After the completion of these greetings and ceremonial rituals, Apollos would say a prayer, and then the meetings would begin, the adults speaking Igbo from that point until the meeting's end.

These gatherings may have been called meetings, but the term would have to be used in the loosest definition of the word possible in order for them to qualify as such; the assemblies were less structured than one would imagine a meeting to be and operated with no real agenda or timetable, which meant they lasted as long as needed until someone would simply say, "Okay. Let's go." Nate recalls, "We would drive all over to go to these 'meetings' like New York, Boston, Worchester, Massachusetts, you name it. You could call them meetings, but it was more like a bunch of people squeezed into the living room of someone's house all yelling at the same time. There really was no structure at all!"

Such Nigerian gatherings were different from the African Christian Fellowship meetings that the Ihedigbos also attended. In addition to being much more structured in their meetings, African Christian Fellowship had a spiritual emphasis, while these Nigerian meetings were more about cultural fellowship and information sharing. However, many of the same expats who attended the Nigerian meetings also attended African Christian Fellowship meetings; after all, son Nate explains, "We are all rooted and grounded by our Christian faith. Christianity is a part of being Igbo, so going to ACF and being Igbo go hand in hand."

The eldest men of the network ran the meetings while the women were responsible for preparing and serving the food, taking in the discussions and whispering their own sidebar commentary among one another as they tended to the affairs of the kitchen. Apollos, as the eldest, always took his place at the head of the meetings. As a child watching his father officiate these affairs, Nate understood that his father occupied this privileged position.

"He was one of the oldest, and he was well respected," he explains, "so he was an elder for both reasons. I was told that my dad was older than he actually was.

The elders' purpose in orchestrating these assemblies of Nigerians throughout the region was always focused on what united them most: Nigeria. Through aggressive dialogue and debate, they would discuss how to improve Nigeria through community building, and they would also update one another on what was happening in their homeland. These years preceded the widespread use of the Internet, and there was not any emphasis on Nigerian current events in American mainstream media. Thus, the group depended on these meetings to provide them with the most recent, up-to-date announcements of what was happening on every level, from the nation all the way down to the village. It was the social networking technology of the day.

"Our sister here returned from the village last week," Apollos would begin at this highly-anticipated time of the meeting because everyone was curious about the state of affairs in their native land. "Can you tell us what you saw and experienced?"

"Well," she would begin with a sigh, feeling both powerful and honored to be the holder of key knowledge that the others in the room desperately longed to hear, "there is news that sister Golibe, the primary teacher from Umuahia has passed on to be with the Lord. She had a stroke in her sleep, and they buried her last month. Many of the school children attended her funeral. Her own children are now living with their dad's sister, their auntie Tobenna in Umuazu while their dad is working in the city. They are having a difficult time and invite your prayers." She would pause for a moment as everyone took in this news, heads shaking in quiet disbelief and sadness. Then she would continue.

"Okorie, the storekeeper's son from *Abame* has married Kamdibe, Belonwu's daughter in a wedding four months ago. Kamdibe is finishing her education at the university and is awaiting approval of her visa application to come and study in Boston.

If she is approved, when she comes, she will need a place for her and her husband to stay, so those of you who live in Boston we ask to discuss who she will stay with when she arrives until they can find a place of her own. "Then Mr. Obioma, the good man we all know from Mbanta was robbed again! Each month, thieves have broken into his house in the village looking for money, and this makes the sixth time this year! Pray for his safety. Also…" the woman would continue her detailed reports, enjoying the spotlight, until she had given every ounce of news she'd learned. Her listeners would listen, carefully attuned to her every word, filing the information away in sacred places in their minds, as this fresh knowledge was their only means of staying intimately connected to the loved ones they'd left behind in Africa.

After the meetings, as they lay on their pillows that night, they would play back the news in their memories, reflecting on and carefully digesting every story that was told. The next day, they would share the news with other Nigerians they knew who were unable to attend the meeting and hear the stories for themselves firsthand, with their own slight embellishments added, of course.

Emeka, David, Nate, and James sat in the kitchen at the kiddie tables. Though they were in junior high and high school at the time, they knew their place among the honored elders in the packed condo apartment or small home who were waiting their turns to shout out their point in the issue currently being debated around the loud, intense conversation or while they sat transfixed listening to the most recent reports out of Nigeria, watching the individual as intently as if they were watching the news on television.

Unlike their parents, uncles, and aunties, the Ihedigbo children did not speak Igbo. They knew words and phrases like "Biko yetum miri?" (May I have some water?) or *ibiala* (welcome) and *ka emesia nu* (good-bye), but that was it—just simple phrases. These phrases they learned as their parents spoke Igbo in the house, and they caught onto the expressions by sheer virtue of repetition, hearing their parents use them over and over again.

The fact that their offspring did not learn Igbo was not due to lack of effort by their parents to teach them; they tried to instruct their children in the language many times. In fact, the Ihedigbos had begun an actual Igbo school at UMass on Saturday mornings at which they would teach the younger Ihedigbo cousins from the Nigerian community how to speak Igbo, and Onyii, Emeka, Nate, David, and James were forced to go. In the class, they would learn numbers, the alphabet, welcomes, and other simple phrases, all things that they remember to this day and cling dearly to as part of their Igbo heritage while regretfully wishing they had taken more time to learn the full language.

While their parents and elders were distracted by the meetings, the Ihedigbo children, unaware of what was being discussed in the other room and, consequently, uninterested, talked and kidded with one another, playing board games, catching up with their cousins, and occasionally engaging in a little mischief.

Nate sat at the miniature table, knees brushing the underside of the small wooden structure to which kids of his age were designated. Restless, his eyes darted across the bite-sized New York kitchen to see if there was anything he might be able to engage to distract him from the impending boredom that was creeping across him, threatening to lull him into a deep sleep. In his search, his eyes landed on the big gray-and-white cooler that held icy cold brown-and-emerald-green bottles of Guinness and Heineken; the constant traffic flow of men coming back and forth from the living room to the kitchen raising the cooler's lid revealed its bounty each time they took a beer.

"David!" Nate whispered to his brother, "Grab me a beer!" David looked at his brother wide-eyed in disbelief at his level of boldness, but he also admired it. Always a willing accomplice to his brother's schemes, he smiled mischievously as he slowly tipped his chair backwards to peek down the hallway that led to the loud living room. The crowd was fully engaged in chaotic discussion, actually arguing in the typical aggressive Igbo fashion, cutting each other off as they each voiced their opinionated positions.

The coast clear, he slowly leaned back, raised the cooler's lid, and quickly grabbed a cold Heineken, hurriedly sliding it across the table to his brother. David and Emeka watched in shock and awe mixed with a bit of envy as their brother used his shirt to twist off the beer's cap and take a small swig.

"Hand me one too! Mom and Dad won't see!" he whispered to David, and David complied, also grabbing one for himself as he grabbed one for Emeka.

The boys entertained themselves by each drinking their very first beer that day as they kept one eye on their parents and one hand on their beers which they hid under the small kiddie table. This was an activity that not only occupied them as they sneaked small sips from their bottles but that occupied them for hours thereafter as their restlessness subsided and their minds danced. They did not particularly like the taste of the beer, but it served its purpose.

Nate, David, and Emeka's scheme was not without witnesses though; at one point, they knew that their uncle who owned the house had seen them secretly turning up their emerald-green bottles with delight. This did not concern them, however, as this particular uncle was cool. He was a New York cabbie who drove like a madman with his hand on the horn nonstop and was always eager to take the boys—who refused to sit in the front seat out of fear—on a trip to see the city whenever they came to town. He was the kind of uncle who would never tell.

The Nigerian network in America represents much more than the standard network of like-minded, similar-purposed individuals that connect themselves for the purpose of sharing information, having their needs met, advancing their personal goals, getting the upper hand on brokering a deal, etc. that we typically see in America. No, the Nigerian network is family, especially when it is discovered that two Nigerians' families are from the same village; based on geographical area alone, they instantly know that they are blood.

When a Nigerian walks into a store and sees a fellow Nigerian man or woman that is even slightly older than him, he greets them with "Hello, Uncle. Hello, Auntie." Mind you, they have never met before, but the rich, strong Nigerian blood that they share has built into it a deep sense of familial connection that makes any Nigerian they meet an instant family member that they would protect, care for, and embrace just as they would those who are their literal biological family members.

The presence of other Nigerians in a city has a strong impact on other Nigerians also moving into the area. For example, James, who recently purchased a home in Houston to live in during the off-season, moved there because there is a larger population of Nigerians in this city, the fourth largest in the U.S., than in other cities. In addition to visiting the city and witnessing its diversity, never-ending events, and attractions, he met his best friend there, fellow Nigerian Amobi Okoye.

"When I went there and met Amobi's family, it was like being around my family," James explains. "Faith-wise, structure-wise, everything was the same, and embracing his dad, mom, and family was like being around my family again!" James enjoyed the instant sense of comfort and familiarity that the Okoye family offered, his home away from home that reminded him of his own Nigerian family. Thus, he bought a home in the same city.

The network of relationship that exists among Nigerians in America is a strong support system that also provides a sense of security for Nigerians, often regarded as aliens in a foreign land despite the fact that they may have been born on American soil. When you are Nigerian in America, even if you are broke and alone, you will always be cared for.

Nate explains, "I can fly to Seattle and be out of money, and I guarantee that my mom will know someone who is Igbo in Seattle that would take me in." This is not an idea based upon mere speculation; it is based upon real-life experience. "When I was in Chicago, my mom had someone who grew up around the same Nigerian village, and I used to go there for meals. Even when I would stay in town by myself for the holidays instead of going home to be with my own family, they would call me and tell me that if I was not going home for the holiday to come over to their house. If you are one of us, you have family that will take care of you wherever you go. It's just part of being Nigerian."

In addition to providing a sense of community, the Nigerian network can provide a trusted source of information that might not otherwise be shared by a typical American. For example, when the Ihedigbos' friend Dr. Daniel Okorafor traveled to the U.S. from Nigeria, he was in for quite a shock. In large part, the reason for this was that he settled in Alabama.

Dr. Okorafor recalls, "Even though we learned in history in Nigeria about how people had been taken from Africa as slaves, I didn't understand what that meant until I arrived in Alabama. I did not discover until I moved to Alabama that the white man thought himself *superior* to the black man! The white man that we had back in Nigeria were missionaries and did not see black men as lesser than they were or as apes. He regarded the black man as a human being. When we moved to Maryland in the north, I learned that this area was better than Alabama in the South when it came to discrimination."

Fortunately as time would go on, Dr. Okorafor would be able to share this vital information with other Nigerians who were planning to move to the United States. Knowing where and where not to settle to have the best possible experience is key for Nigerians.

THE EYE-OPENING
JOURNEY BACK TO NIGERIA

"Okay, kids, we have an announcement to make. We're going to Nigeria! We're going to take you back to see the country that you are from, and we are going to visit the villages we grew up in with your grandmothers and aunties and uncles and cousins, and you will finally get the chance to…" James's mother and father's enthusiastic words faded out, and he could no longer hear their voices, as they were now falling on deaf ears as his face became hot and his heart sank. He could only picture in my mind himself running up and down the shiny hardwood basketball court, colorful lines marking the shooting and zone lines, and the crowds cheering him on, calling his name. He was a sophomore, and this was the middle of the basketball season.

"Are you kidding me?" He broke in, trying not to sound panicked. "It's the middle of the basketball season! I *can't* go!"

"You'll just have to miss this part of the season, James," his parents carefully explained. "This is a family trip, and it is important that you go to see the country that we came from. You must stay in touch with your culture and your people in Nigeria. Believe us, you will enjoy it, and missing basketball is not the end of the world. Your team will just have to do without you."

James was sad. Even more than not being able to improve his averages and play against some tough rivals scheduled for the basketball season, he was most saddened at the prospect that he would have to abandon his team for the time that he was away; they played as a unit. Nevertheless, he held a nervous anticipation for what lay ahead of him in Nigeria, a land about which he had only heard from his parents and his aunties and uncles.

It was 1992, and the Ihedigbos were making their first trip as a family back to Nigeria. David and Nate settled into their seats on the airplane, craning their necks to try to lay eyes on their family members seated several sections ahead of them. They were tired because they had stayed up the entire night before in excited anticipation of their first trip back to Nigeria. Once the airplane had taken off and reached a nice altitude, the flight attendant soon came by with the beverage cart. "What can I get you to drink, sir?" she asked.

David was tall for his age. Though he was only eleven years old, he was already nearly six feet tall, so he looked older than he was. His seat partner Nate was thirteen years old at the time, and the same was true of him. Despite being underage, they both ordered a beer and happily reclined their seats in comfort. After all, they were over international waters, so U.S. rules did not apply, and in Nigeria, there was no drinking age. To the two boys, this meant they were not breaking the law. Thus, on the plane ride over the waters, they continued to enjoy beer after beer until they were sufficiently buzzed. Had their parents known, they would have killed the two boys, but Apollos and Rose had stayed up the entire night too, so David and Nate were sure they would be sleeping. This trip was getting off to a fun start!

During the breaks between watching movies, reading magazines, and watching the vast expanse of sky just outside the plane's window, the two boys began to think of what lay ahead of them when they landed in Nigeria. Half asleep and half awake, through their minds raced of the many gatherings they'd had with their Nigerian uncles, aunts, and cousins in the States. *Would Nigeria be just like that*, they wondered. When they announced that they would soon be traveling to Africa, people told them that they would love the experience, but would this be true?

Because of the close fellowship that the Ihedigbo family shared with other Nigerians in the States from the Nigerian house meetings to the African Christian fellowship, the Ihedigbo children carried with them at least *some* notions of what Nigeria would be like.

"One thing I expected to encounter was the smell—the musty Igbo smell...the African smell," says Nate. "Even in the States, my uncles would always have this smell that we just know as the Igbo smell. We couldn't stand it, but I expected to encounter it at another level once I got to Nigeria." In addition to this, Nate expected to feel the pride of his people in his home country.

"I'm very proud to have 100 percent Nigerian blood," he explains. "And I was looking forward to being surrounded for the first time in my life by other people who were pure-blooded Nigerians—not watered down—and proud of it."

While Nate had more concrete ideas of what he might expect, David was not so sure. "My parents had told me stories of the village and having to walk thirty miles with buckets of water on their heads, but each time they told the story, the miles got longer and longer, so I didn't know *what* to believe!" he explains.

Without any clear expectations of what he might encounter, David thought to himself, *I don't know what I am getting into on this trip!* Besides having a mental image of dirt everywhere and being surrounded by people with the Igbo smell, the only thing he could actually say he expected was to be overwhelmed.

Perhaps most meaningful of all, the Ihedigbo siblings looked forward to finally seeing the villages that Apollos and Rose had told them about constantly; from the time they were born, they'd heard about the village, the village, the village. Now they would finally get the chance to lay eyes on the village, to see if the picture they'd painted in their minds actually matched the reality of what existed in Nigeria. The village was significant to these siblings because it held a significant key aspects of their identity that had been hidden until now, aspects that could only released by setting foot on the soil from which they were directly descended.

Since they had been in America, it had been a lifelong dream for Apollos and Rose to expose their children to the village once the children had reached an age where they could appreciate it. "My parents wanted us to see where they grew up because they thought that seeing it at a young age would help to shape us," he explained. "They thought it would cause us to want to work harder in life. When they talked about taking us to their village, my parents would say, 'You have to know where you came from in order to know where you are going.'"

After the twenty-four-hour flight, now completely sobered up and ready to experience their homeland, Nate and David picked up their carry-on belongings and disembarked the plane.

David remembers vividly the first scene his mind captured upon arriving in Nigeria. "When we landed, it seemed like it was out of a movie!" he explains. "Before we got off the plane, the flight attendant announced, 'It's a beautiful 112 degrees outside and sunny!' *One hundred twelve degrees*? As soon as I got off the plane, I was sweating. We disembarked outside and had to walk across the terminal into the airport, and just crossing over this area my skin was seriously burning—I thought I was getting sunburned! Instantly, I discovered that my deodorant didn't work in this kind of weather, so I wouldn't even try to put it on for the rest of the trip. Then there was no air-conditioning in the airport. I knew this was going to be a hard trip!"

All of the siblings had been warned about the heat—"another kind of hot, scorching heat," as Nate describes it. He also discovered this to be exactly the case as he disembarked the plane that touched down on the tarmac, waves of heat radiating from the ground's hot surface.

James recalls, "I remember getting there and instantly you could feel the unbearable heat. Right there at the airport, it hit you like a ton of bricks, not only the heat, but the smell in the thick, dense air which was very different. I was like, 'Wow!' The people looked and smelled different, you couldn't just sit there and take a deep breath, it was so thick and dense. It was tough."

Though Emeka was not on this trip with the family, his testimony of landing in Nigeria on a past trip is consistent with that of his siblings.

"Walking off the plane is literally like stepping onto another planet. It's drastically different from the U.S. Imagine landing in a spaceship in another place, and the first thing that strikes you as you breathe in the hot oxygen is the smell—not a bad smell, but a combination of earthy copper, dust, and people. Over the years, I've come to associate the smell with adventure," he explains.

On a later trip to Nigeria in 1995, with only his mother and his sister, Onyii, Emeka recalls one such adventure that happened after the trio landed. Before they even got out of the Nigerian airport, he got his first taste of Nigerian corruption.

"Come up here, Emeka, and give me your passport," Rose said as he stood at the customs desk. She turned towards her daughter who had already gone through customs and reminded her to put her passport back into her bag and zip it for security. From underneath the shiny black brim of his hat, the uniformed customs agent's eyes watched the seventeen-year-old Emeka unzip his bag and remove his passport. He laid it on the desk and turned to his mother.

"Mom, can we go get something to eat once we get in the car? Because I'm really hungry, and—" Emeka's conversation with his mother was interrupted by the customs agent.

"Where is your passport?" he asked Emeka in a strong, bold voice. Emeka turned his head back towards the counter and no longer saw his passport. He looked down at his bag, which was still unzipped from its removal.

"What do you mean? I just took it out and put it up here. I gave it to you already!" he replied, confused. He was sure he had taken it out of his backpack and handed it over.

"No, you didn't give me your passport, and you cannot get into the country without a passport. Where is your passport?" Emeka looked at his mother, bewildered.

"Mom, I swear I put it up there. It was sitting right there!" he said. Rose stepped up to the desk.

"What is this? My son says he gave you his passport," she insisted.

"Where is my Merry Christmas?" the customs agent said under low breath, not making eye contact with her.

"What did you say?" she demanded strongly as she leaned her head down to make eye contact with the corrupt official. She knew the ways of her country, but she was not going to let him get away with it so easily.

"Where is my Merry Christmas?" he repeated again, nonchalantly shuffling the papers on his desk. He was in no hurry to pass these guests through his customs gate. He could wait all day.

"I don't believe you. I don't know what you want from us! This is our country, and we are just coming to visit—" she began to protest, but her words were soon cut short as he held fast to his position.

"Where…is…my…Merry…Christmas?" This time, he stared at her intently in the eyes, enunciating each word as a signal that he was not backing down. These were American passports, she was clearly Igbo, and he knew she knew the drill. Indeed she did. Rose reached into her bag for her wallet from which she counted out several bills. Passing the money across the counter, Emeka's passport reappeared in an instant. The customs agent stamped it, placed it on the counter, said "Have a nice trip!" Then as if nothing had ever happened, he called out to the next person in line, "Next!"

From this, Emeka learned an essential lesson about travel to Nigeria. In your budgeting, allot for the traditional travel expenses like airline tickets and lodging, but you must also have an expense category for bribes. Without it, you would have a hard time in Nigeria. Greasing the wheels by paying bribes was simply a way of life here. Like it or not, this was the Nigerian way.

Fortunately, the Ihedigbos on this trip suffered no such misadventure as they easily collected their belongings and made their way to the airport. After retrieving their bags and successfully navigating their way through customs, the family stepped out of the airport to see their uncles waiting for them. The scene was a busy one outside with vendors selling various types of handmade arts, jewelry, and other wares, ready to pounce on souvenir-hungry travelers who had money to spend. "Don't buy anything here, and do not take anything!" Rose called out protectively to her naïve group of travelers.

Prior to packing for the trip, Rose had advised her children very specifically: "Do not wear any expensive clothes, or you will be an easy target because they will know you have money. Wear your regular clothes, and do not bring any more than $20 to spend. The exchange rate fluctuates up and down a little, but typically in Nigeria, if you add two zeroes to the amount of U.S. money you have, twenty U.S. dollars will become two thousand Nigerian naira. That will be all you will need to spend."

When it came to what to wear, the siblings heeded their mother's words. However, when it came to the money they would bring along to spend, they had their own mind. Each of the boys had summer jobs or other sources of money, so they brought a little more: David $100, Nate $100, and James $50. Almost as if she could smell the U.S. dollars in their pockets, an old woman walked up to David and offered him a ribbon. Heeding his mother's instructions, he gave a "No, thank you" shake of the head and began to walk away. Put off by the refusal of her wares, the old woman began to yell at him in Igbo until Rose, being the protective mother that she was, rushed over and demanded that the woman leave her son alone.

"Don't give my sons anything!" she warned the old lady in her own strong Igbo, unintimidated by the look the woman gave her. With the inability to speak Igbo, the siblings did not know what their mother said, but they knew it worked. The old lady walked away. The advantaged Americans instantly realized that they were at a disadvantage in Igboland.

"Not knowing the native language made us foreigners in our own native country, and that was very weird," remembers David.

Once the family's bags had been stuffed into their uncle's vehicle, they drove away from the airport—but not before David witnessed something that sent him into a panic.

"The military runs Nigeria," he says. "They walk around with big, huge AK47 machine guns. When we were leaving the airport, I know I saw this: an army guy had a civilian on the side of the road, and he shot the guy and killed him right there! I could not believe that this happened right in front of my eyes. I yelled out to everyone in the car, 'Look! Did you just see that? Did you see that?' but nobody else saw. My mom said that nothing had happened to the guy, that they were just going to make him pay a bribe, but I know what I saw. The place was crazy!"

Raised all their lives in the comforts of America, modest as they were in a middle-class Massachusetts home, the Ihedigbo children who set foot on Nigerian soil for the first time in their memories (Onyii, Emeka, and David were very young when they left) were in for quite a culture shock. Everything about Nigeria was waiting to offend their now-middle-class Westernized sensibilities.

Nate watched closely as his mother Rose carefully counted out the naira for the short plane ride her family would take from Lagos to Port Harcourt, Rivers State. By American standards, this plane would have been retired in a bunker somewhere, for it appeared to have seen its better days. "It was a rickety plane that made you pray for your life," Nate remembers. "It was like you had to get out and push the plane to make it go, and it bounced you all around in your seat as it flew through the air!"

Travel to more remote places in a country that is not fully developed can be challenging, as there were more legs to the trip after this second flight. After the plane landed in Port Harcourt, the family hired a driver to transport them to Umuahia, the capital of Abia state. He picked up the family of seven and their luggage in a Volvo station wagon and transported them to the home of Rose's sister, Mary Akumah.

Mary's Nigerian home was like most other Nigerian middle-class homes, but completely unlike any the Ihedigbo children ever saw in the States. The home and its property were surrounded by a tall, thick concrete security wall that was painted white, and cemented to the top of the wall were large shards of broken glass, thick barbed wire, or pointed poles to prohibit potential intruders from scaling the walls to infiltrate the family's compound. Entrance to these well-secured quarters could only be gained through a huge metal access gate that was opened by a worker only after he verified a guest's identity. It was through this gate that the old Volvo station wagon creaked, exposing the children to a surprisingly nice home with ceramic tile floors.

Upon their arrival, they were welcomed by their aunt and her husband, and they stayed overnight in the home, glad to finally rest from the activity of their first day's adventures in Nigeria.

The children woke up excited the next day, for this is the day that they would drive into town where their father's condo was, and after getting settled, their journey towards their father's village would begin. Apollos kept a very nice contemporary condo on Bonnie Street in Umuahia. Complete with a driver, a door man, running water, and a generator when the unstable electric grid went out, this three-bedroom abode on the third floor of a residential building in the heart of Umuahia, provided a satisfactory and comfortable living.

Early in the morning, as soon as the sun rose, early-rising Ihedigbos stepped just outside of the huge living room onto the balcony where the people watching would begin. As the condo boasted a clear view of the local Fanta factory three blocks away, they would curiously watch people gather around the factory gate with cases of empty bottles on their head. The people would exchange the empty bottles for full ones as soon as the factory opened. The balcony also provided a bird's-eye view of the market just blocks away abuzz with a wide variety of Nigerian foods and products as well as traditional Western goods.

Taking an *okada* motorcycle ride to the market, they would return laden down with the same types of goods that they would find at any Western mall. The Ihedigbo boys were surprised at the items they were able to score in such an unlikely place. Their brother Emeka had previously gone ahead of them and come back home with some nice shoes— Jordans, in fact—that he'd bought in the Nigerian market. However, the young shoppers had no idea that they would find things like these! There were movies that were still in the theatres, rap from American artists like Jay Z, and more. There was even an electronics section right there in the marketplace on the street, much to their surprise.

Riding through town in the direction of the Apollos' village, some of the roads were paved, but most had huge potholes that had to be navigated with care; and even with care, if any part of the vehicle's tires touched one of these craters in the road, the whole car would rock dramatically back and forth, causing its passengers to have to brace themselves to avoid potential injury.

Once the car reached the outskirts of town, the car was forced to brave a different terrain as it climbed up and down unpaved hills made of red clay dirt. After successfully navigating these roads and nearing the village, the off-road adventure *really* began—the car turned off the main dirt road and into huge fields of tall grass, mowing a path through the grass as it slowly made its way through the bumpy landscape towards the village. Despite the ride, the Ihedigbo children were not as apprehensive as they were eager to see what lay ahead.

As they rode, a million questions quietly danced through their heads. Would the images of "the village" that their parents constantly referred to match the village to which they were headed for the very first time? Would it be safe? Would the people like them? Would they be able to communicate with them since they didn't speak Igbo? Though the children did not give voice to these questions, they did voice their amazement at what they saw as they rode. For their parents, this was home; however, for the children, what they encountered on the ride to the village was like being on safari, though the objects of their amazement were people instead of animals.

"Look at that lady walking with that big bowl on her head! How does she *do* that?" one would exclaim.

"No, look at *that* lady over there with that tall stack of bags on her head! It's almost taller than *she* is!" another would point out.

"Wait! Look at that house! It's only one step up from a refu-gee camp. It's not even fully enclosed. Do people really live there, Dad? What do they do when it rains?" they marveled at the severe poverty they were witnessing for the first time in their lives.

The family arrived in the village of Umuawa at night, so the fact that there were no streetlights was immediately highlighted in the awareness of the Ihedigbo children who rode along in the backseat of the car, wide-eyed and unsure of what lay ahead. The car creaked as it bounced down an unpaved dirt road towards Apollos' family village. In the darkness, the headlights of the small car was the only light available to guide them to their destination.

As they pulled in to the small cluster of houses in the com-pound that Apollos once called home, houses without electricity, dozens of kerosene lanterns seemed to emerge out of nowhere, lighting the thick darkness, lighting the huge smiles of curious, unfamiliar faces that seemingly floated out of small dark homes to greet them. James turned to look at his brothers Nate and David in disbelief. *I want to go home*, he thought to himself. *This is too much.*

Little did he know that his brother David was experiencing the same type of internal crisis. He recalls, "I was in culture shock when I saw where they grew up. I thought I was in hell! I was like, do we really have to endure *three weeks* of this?"

Nate, however, was not as apprehensive as his brothers as they exited the car in the circle of houses within the compound. "We stepped out of the car, and at first, everyone just looked at us, and then they just started running up to us and hugging us. My dad had told them in advance that we were coming, so they knew who we were when we got there," Nate recalls. This newfound attention in the midst of his newly discovered family members was something he relished. He explains, "I felt like a celebrity... kind of on top of the world! We were so Americanized when we got there, and I had on a blue Nike tank top and a full Nike suit, so kids were touching and feeling my clothes and shoes. We also had Sony Walkmans, and the kids were saying, 'Let me get this! Let me get this!' as they pointed to our Walkmans, our watches—whatever we had."

Apollos and Rose had prepared their children for such requests, and the young Ihedigbos came prepared for them. "Our parents told us to bring things that we could give. We had our allowances, plus I had picked cucumbers, so I had money with me. I didn't know that I might not come back with my Walkman and watch, but I did come prepared to give some money because I could always get more money when I returned to America. Seeing how needy they were, and knowing that these kids were actually my blood, I basically said, 'For love, I got you,' and I gave them money," says Nate.

Nate's generous heart and love for his people who were relegated to such poverty led him to give away most of what he'd brought along with him on the trip. He explains, "One family had a maid who lived there but didn't get paid, so I gave her kids stuff. Our cousins our age were the first to welcome us, so we gave them stuff." By the time he completed his Nigerian adventure, Nate had little left in his bag; for recognizing his relative privilege, he gave it away to those in greater need.

David also felt compelled to give of what he had to his relatives in the village. "The big story was that my dad was the second oldest son and he had five siblings. Though they were friendly, I saw some jealousy on the faces of the people that wondered why he got this opportunity and they did not. They had nothing. I gave a lot of people money. Even though I'd brought only one hundred U.S. dollars., it was ten thousand naira, and that was a lot of money for Nigeria. It wasn't a big deal though because it wasn't going to break my bank. I knew what I was going back to—a comfortable life and more money—and that they could use this money better as they struggled to make it from month to month. Not only was it the right thing to do, but my dad was such a giving person, and I am a reflection of my father. Something in me just wanted to help."

The family stayed with relatives in Apollos's village of Umuawa during their time there. It was a drastic change in lifestyle, staying in the village, and to use the term "culture shock" at the way they had to temporarily live would be an understatement.

"I remember complaining about the shower with ice-cold water," explains James of his experience. "In order to take a hot bath, you had to boil hot water, pour it in a bucket, splash the water on yourself, soap up, and rinse off with that same bucket of water."

Added to this is Nate's recollection that the electricity in the compound was not constant.

"Electricity in the compound was on for fifteen minutes, then off for an hour, then on for thirty minutes, then off for an hour, and so on," he recalls. Those were the first of many experiences that gave the Ihedigbo siblings an immediate sense of gratitude to God—one of his and his siblings' greatest takeaways from this trip—and to their parents for providing a safe, warm, comfortable place for them to live back in the states.

As they gradually accepted the fact that this is where they were from and that this is where their mother and father were born and raised, things became easier. They embraced Nigeria. They were Nigerian, and this was their home, the "real" Nigeria that they had never known, complete with foreign smells, foreign foods, foreign transportation, foreign people, foreign places, and foreign dangers. Over the course of one or two days, the young Ihedigbos adapted to their surroundings, and soon, despite its being so foreign, they loved their home country so much that when all was said and done, they did not want to leave.

As soon as they'd arrived in Nigeria and prepared to go into the village, Rose and Apollos were careful to have a slightly uncomfortable yet necessary talk with their sons and daughter before their children set out on their adventures.

"When you go into the village, if someone offers you anything, do not eat it. No matter how much they insist or how nice they are, do not eat it." Apollos's voice was grave and serious as he spoke to his children in his thick Nigerian accent, making the hairs on their neck stand up with this advice.

"Even if it's family?" an astonished son asked.

"Yes, even if it's family. Especially if it's family." Apollos replied.

"Why, Dad?" one of the boys bravely asked.

"Because they could poison you, so unless we are with you or unless you are at a hotel, do not eat anything," Rose explained.

"Why would they want to poison us? We didn't do anything," another of the boys added.

"They love you, but they hate you for what you have and how you live. They wish they were there and had the kind of money that you do, so do not eat or drink anything they put before you. Just say 'No, thank you,' and refuse it," Rose answered.

"If the top is already open on a drink, like a soda, you do not drink it. Drink nothing unless you open it yourself," Apollos chimed in. "Do you understand?" he asked his children. They silently nodded in unanimous agreement, visibly stunned at the potential dangers that had been revealed to them in only one brief conversation with their parents.

Nate remembers, "When they told us not to eat anything because some could try to poison us, it made me paranoid—a *lot*! There was definitely a level of shadiness that existed in this place that we didn't know about until now, so we had to take precautions. It was a real danger."

After getting over the shock of the potential dangers, however, the boys, mindful of the precautions that were to guide their behavior, were ready to hit the streets. James remembers, "We would wake up in the morning, get dressed, tell our mom and dad we were leaving, and be out the door. Mom would tell us to be back at a certain time because she was concerned about our safety, but we were with our cousin, so everybody knew there was less of a concern; he would see after us. We'd be gone all day long and then come back at night after having a great time with the other kids. It was a blast!"

One of the most fascinating things about Nigeria is its transport system. As with many underdeveloped countries, Nigerian transport does not operate according to the organized, orderly fashion that America does. No, in Nigeria, it is every man for himself on the road that results in a dangerous dance of cars and trucks, horns firing off at a minimum of fifty horns per second, all vying for prime position on the roads, mostly unpaved dirt ones, with seemingly hundreds of un-helmeted motorcycle-taxi drivers weaving in and out of the traffic, so close that the motorcyclists and the riders that cling on to them from behind commonly bump your car (just as the cars commonly bump them) or even reach out their hands to hold onto the neighboring car to brace themselves as they squeeze through two-feet-wide openings to deliver the two or three brave passengers, also sans helmets, that are riding with them to their destination.

In Nigeria, these taxis, which are bigger than a scooter but smaller than a motorcycle, are called *okadas*. Their drivers would rig up the motors to make the tiny machines go really fast—up to seventy miles per hour—and while they would definitely be considered dangerous by more conservative Western standards, the Ihedigbo boys found them simply irresistibly fun as they embarked on their Nigerian adventure. On one such daily adventure, however, they suffered a dangerous moment that could have been much worse than it turned out to be.

Any seasoned okada rider knows that when you exit a motorcycle taxi, you exit on the opposite side of the muffler. As the cycle has been humming all day to deliver its passengers to their destinations, both the engine and its various components become blazing hot from use and from the rays that reflect off of it from the hot African sun. As James, Nate, David, and a couple of their cousins hailed several okadas to take them into town, their only concern was who they would see and the delicious food they would eat at the hotel they were headed to watch a popular soccer game.

After about fifteen minutes of navigating around potholes and weaving through the thick traffic, they arrived at their destination. Each of the young men exited the proper way—dismounting the okada on the side opposite of the muffler; however, Nate had forgotten this critical rule of Nigerian transport and got off on the wrong side. A scream filled the air as heads turned to see Nate grab his leg that had been burned badly by the hot muffler, and his cousins and brothers rushed to his side. While they did not allow the horror of the sight of Nate's badly seared leg show on their faces, they all knew that this was a pretty serious injury. They carefully rushed him inside of the hotel where staff members cleaned the wound. Later on, when their mother saw the wound, she put salt on it, allowing it to suck the moisture right on out of the wound. Only by God's grace was the wound not as grave as it could have been.

The gang eventually made it to the city's nicest hotel and helped themselves to a table at the restaurant. As they sat, their cousin pointed out the governor of the state that sat at a nearby table. As they sat chatting happily, taking in their nice surroundings, the waiter came to the table.

"What are these kids doing here?" he asked in Igbo via translation of their cousin. "Get up at once if you guys are not spending any money!" he continued, again via translation.

David would show this cocky waiter who he was dealing with. "Tell him to let me see a menu," he instructed his cousin. His cousin asked for a menu in Igbo.

"I'll take three of these, three of these, four of these, "David pointed out item after item on the menu, ordering up the finest in food and drinks.

"Oh, yeah? How are you going to pay for this?" demanded the waiter through their translating cousin. David reached into his pocket, pulling out a thick wad of Nigerian cash.

"Do you take tens, fifties, and hundreds?" he asked smugly, taking delight in the waiter's newly humbled disposition. That day, the boys feasted well and even sent over a big bottle of Remy Martin cognac to the governor's table. They had an amazing time and were really learning to enjoy Nigeria.

Despite Nate's unfortunate burn injury, his memories of he and his brothers and cousin's adventures were all good. Speaking of the fun they had on the okadas during their trip makes him break out into a smile, even as he recounts the stories today.

"Man, I *loved* riding around on the okadas. They were awesome!" he reminisces. "We changed about twenty American dollars into a fat wad of money and rode around balling big, taking okadas all over the place, tipping big. My cousin Uche Ihedigbo who was with us would talk them down off their price, and then we would tell the one driver to go get his friends to take us around. We felt completely safe because we trusted our cousin and he spoke Igbo. He was awesome to us."

Of course, hanging out with his well-off American cousins was a benefit for Uche as well. He'd gotten to his American cousins first, and thus, he was the first they'd embraced. As a result, he became their tour guide and had the customary the honor of showing them around and introducing them to the city. It didn't hurt that they carried lots of money, so everything was on his cousins—food, drink, and entertainment at the hotels, which were set up like clubs, you name it. Thus, this honorary host reaped benefits and held a position that his other cousins in the village would have given anything to occupy.

Spending time in Nigeria with their cousin Uche as their tour guide turned out to be quite a wise move, because as a local, he knew how to navigate the murky waters of the police system. There was no real, legitimate security force in place, and those who are in place to protect and serve are known for their high levels of corruption. In fact, the police are known to stop taxis and carloads full of people at road blocks that they randomly set up in the middle of the street, forcing each person to pay something in order to pass.

"Okay, everybody pay up!" the policemen would say. To not pay meant that the car could be detained and inconvenienced for quite sometime, perhaps even an hour or more. For this reason, in addition to the potential threat of kidnapping for ransom, which was an especially big risk for Americans, public figures, and Nigerians who were well off, Uche encouraged them to never go out at night.

The Ihedigbo boys soon learned that not everyone was desperately poor in Nigeria. This was especially true in the case of the *eze*, or chief, who was for all intents and purposes the president of the village community. The boys' cousin knew the sons and daughters of the eze in Apollos' village, so they went over to their house.

The eze's house was always in its own compound and stood out from its surroundings because it had the finest of goods, including cars, satellite television, and other amenities fit for a king in the midst of a poor rural village. As the boys pulled up to the gate on their okadas, they were amazed at the stark difference in living conditions between the eze and the rest of the compound. Here, the gate was about fifteen feet high, and inside there was plush green grass everywhere—not like the dirt yards in the rest of the village.

"It looked like it was a house straight off of *MTV Cribs*!" describes David.

The house was humongous, very modern and contemporary. In the driveway sat several of the finest luxury cars. When they entered, all guests were asked to remove their shoes at the door; this was first for them in Africa. Being in this home was like being back in the U.S. for the boys.

Nate recalls of being in the eze's home, "I was amazed that at the eze's house, you could watch ESPN Sports Center there. Wow!"

The boys were introduced to the family, starting with the eze's son whom their cousin knew and then the eze's beautiful daughters. Though they were wealthy, the young man and his sisters were quite down to earth. The group, comprised of the Ihedigbo boys, their cousin, and the eze's son and daughters would go on to spend time together, enjoying the freedom of being young and carefree as they made their way through the city, swimming, sharing meals at the hotel restaurant, and getting to know each other a little better.

Of all of the great stories that the Ihedigbo share about their trip to Nigeria, one in particular was quite unsettling. As with travel to many African countries from the U.S., travelers are instructed to begin a course of antimalarial antibiotics beginning two weeks prior to departure. Then the medicine should continue to be taken while in the guest country to avoid contracting malaria. In the Ihedigbo family, everyone complied with the doctor's orders—except James. He had chosen to wait until one week before the family's departure for Nigeria before he began his regimen of antibiotics.

On one particularly hot evening, David, James, and Nate decided to sleep outside on the balcony. Sleeping outside in the nighttime's cool breeze was not an unusual thing in Africa. The next morning, David and Nate woke up itching. Looking down, they each had a few mosquito bites, but they were nothing major at all. As their eyes shifted over to their brother, however, the sight was terrifying: James was covered with red mosquito bites all over his body. Scrambling over their blankets, they called his name, "James!" but he did not respond.

"Mom, Dad! Come quick! It's James!" they called into the condo where the rest of the family was just beginning to wake and mill around. Rose rushed onto the balcony and saw her son laying there covered in mosquito bites. Instinctively, she felt his forehead. The intense heat radiating from his body instantly told her what she needed to know.

"James has contracted malaria. Quick! Go get the antimalaria pills out of my bag!" she commanded her sons.

Together, in one of the scariest moments any of them had encountered, they began to force-feed James antimalaria pills. Though his fever began to dissipate after a while, the young man was bedridden, and it took about three days for him to recover enough to be back on his feet. Once they knew that their baby brother would be okay, Nate and David let him have it.

"You're such an idiot, James! You should have been taking your medicine! We have been riding all over the city on the okadas with our cousin having all kinds of fun. This has been the best three days of our vacation, and you missed it *all*!" Leave it up to brothers to rub things in.

The three-week trip that Apollos and Rose took their children on to Nigeria would forever leave an indelible impression on the lives of the young people. Being able to see it and experience it firsthand paled in comparison to the stories about their upbringing in the village that they'd previously told their children. Their son David summarizes what is in many regards the collective takeaway for the group.

"Just seeing where my parents came from and the few resources they had changed my life. It showed me that by living in America, I have everything at my fingertips, so there is no way for me to fail at anything, whether school or business. When I feel like my life is difficult, I now think about my parents growing up in the village. My life is chump change compared to what they had to do. They had to walk miles and miles to get water, and I just have to walk to a faucet. It makes me grateful and makes me want to instill the same principles to my children. It makes me want to do greater. If my parents could take themselves from Nigeria, travel to another country with nothing, earn doctorates, and build a good life for their children, from where I am right now, I should be able to build the largest franchise known to man. That is how great of an accomplishment they made when they came here. They showed me that the sky is the limit!"

About his rich Nigerian experience, James explains, "In the states, we had a strong community of Nigerians we all grew up with, and Mom and Dad educated us on our culture, so it wasn't like we weren't familiar with Nigerian people. Going to Nigeria and learning about Nigerian people there versus in the U.S. was just different. You would meet Nigerians there and see how they acted and interacted, and you would say, 'So *that's* why I am the way I am,' especially when it comes to my levels of hard work, determination, and being driven to achieve. What I'd seen in myself, I saw in other Nigerians on my trip there, and it helped me to understand that much more about myself. That's just the way we're built. Being in Nigeria was like looking at yourself in a mirror because it made you say, 'Wow! That guy looks familiar… he acts *just* like me!'"

On the occasions when they walked through the market devouring their *suya*, spicy seasoned meat on a stick, and browsing the hundreds of colorful rickety makeshift booths that flanked them on both sides with people vying for products at the best price, the boys would marvel at the displays of aggression in the public market as the negotiations ensued.

"There were a lot of people arguing loudly in the market," Nate explains. "It looked like they would be on the verge of fighting, but they never did. The same thing happened on the buses and transportation, but nothing violent ever happens. We learned that they're just *super* aggressive in this culture. It's part of how we are as Nigerians."

The experiences the young Ihedigbos encountered and the lessons they learned from this monumental trip would last them a lifetime.

NATAC AND LIFE BACK
IN NIGERIA

Before Apollos and Rose Ihedigbo ever left their home nation of Nigeria in the late seventies and early eighties, they knew that they would travel to the U.S., become educated, and then return to Nigeria to start a school. This was a plan that was concrete—resolute. They never second-guessed it. Never in light of the challenging circumstances they faced did they ever consider deviating from the plan, not even for a moment. The reason: they knew that God had given them this plan, and in the proper season, He would release them to bring it to pass. In the meantime, they would do all they could to prepare for that great day, praying that the Lord would give them favor. One day in 1999, God spoke.

Almost twenty years after all of the education, preparation, and praying, Apollos felt a release in his spirit that now was the season to go back to Nigeria and build the school of which he'd dreamt for so long. At this, he took a sabbatical from his job at the University of Massachusetts as the associate director of the Committee for the Collegiate Education of Black and other Minority Students (CCEBMS) and launched the plan that would soon be established as NATAC: the Nigerian-American Technological and Agricultural College.

"I've looked through our financing options, Apollos, and it just doesn't seem feasible right now," said Patrick Smith, the president of the board of directors Apollos had established to assist with the establishment of NATAC on the U.S. end. There was another NATAC board of directors over in Nigeria. "We just don't have the funds," he said as he looked down at the spreadsheets that lay before him one more time.

"Listen, Patrick. God wants this to happen, so it's going to happen. I know it doesn't look like it, but it is going to come to pass," said Apollos. He'd known his friend Patrick for a while now, having attended the same church with him for years. Patrick was also a music teacher who had taught Emeka and Onyii in school. If there was one thing he knew about his friend, it was that he would always be the voice of practicality while Apollos always provided the voice of vision and creativity.

"If you say it will happen, it will happen," Patrick said. He believed what he was saying because his friend had often spoken to him of his covenant with God: if God would allow him to study in the U.S. and earn his degree, he would come back to help his people with education someday. God had been faithful to doing his part, and he was confident that as Apollos endeavored to fulfill his part of the covenant, God would be with him. Apollos took a sip of his diet soft drink, shifted in his seat, leaned forward, and looked Patrick squarely in the face.

"It *will* happen, Pat!" Apollos affirmed. "I know it will happen because I believe that God has sent me here to fulfill His word. It's purpose. It's destiny. God will provide a way for NATAC to have this curriculum. It is the best one for our program, and we will have the best," said Apollos with a confident smile. Sometimes it was necessary to comfort his business-minded friend like this. He sat back in his chair under the shaded porch outside of his home as he watched the Sunday afternoon sun wash over the large open fields that sat near his home. Patrick had full awareness of the funds they had available, but Apollos had full awareness of what his God would do.

Perhaps the biggest challenge in starting NATAC was raising the funds from the United States to go back to Nigeria and start the school. The ones who offered the most assistance in the endeavor was the College Church in Northampton. As soon as Apollos raised the vision to the trustees of the church, they bought into it. While offering support in prayers was a welcomed and very necessary thing, equally necessary was funding, which they also offered. The church announced Apollos's vision to the congregation, and soon after, they designated Apollos as one of their missionaries that would be supported by a missionary fund that still continues to support the school today even after Apollos's passing.

After obtaining the initial monies to get the school started, the second biggest challenge did not come until Apollos was on the ground doing the legwork in Nigeria: he needed to find a building that would house the new school. Driving up and down the busy streets in the most desirable and heavily populated areas of town, Apollos considered building after building, weighing the pros and cons of each. Finally, after a considerable amount of time spent searching, he found just the right one: a three-story building at 1 Item Street in Umuahia.

Walking into the new NATAC building, it was clear that whoever had organized the place meant business. On the first floor were the administrative offices and five computer-filled classrooms, as one of the school's primary focuses was on computer technology. Colorful posters hung at eye level to advertise many of the school's upcoming courses decorated the walls throughout the narrow hallways.

The second floor of the building featured a science lab for general science and biological studies. In addition to teaching computer technology and the sciences, the school was equipped to teach basics like English and math. Most often, these classes were reserved for students that had educational deficiencies going into college, allowing them to be retrained in the basics that would secure a spot to study in a four-year college or university.

Finally, on the third floor of the building was the school's library. There, one could find books of every topic and from every genre, many of which were donated by the University of

Massachusetts. NATAC remained in this impressive three-story building until 2008, when the organization had to downsize and change locations as a result of escalating rents.

After Apollos had done the most important legwork towards getting NATAC established, which included locating, renovating, and equipping a facility with the necessary technological and learning resources, it was time to engage a level of challenge that he had been dreading all along—the corrupt and highly bureaucratic red tape of Nigeria's educational and governmental system. Due to the high levels of bribery and corruption that are pervasive in these systems, they can often be quite difficult and time consuming to navigate; however, in order to be cleared for operation, he would have to register for and pass a facility inspection and licensure process. Fortunately, the Lord provided, giving Apollos the favor he needed to navigate through the necessary channels and procedures, and now he was clear to open soon.

The next order on the agenda was to hire staff. The hiring was not so difficult—there were enough capable Nigerians from which he could choose to be instructors. The Lord led Apollos to several loyal, faithful, and Spirit-filled job seekers that would eventually still remain there today. Though various staff members and instructors have come and gone over the years, the most key position—the site administrator—has been a NATAC fixture since the school first opened. All of the school's staff, from administrators to instructors, has remained Nigerians.

The following step towards getting the new school up and running was to establish a strategic approach to marketing and advertising the new NATAC. There was no clear system of how to advertise and get the word out about open registration at the new school. In the absence of radio, television, and newspaper advertising, all of which were too costly to advertise in, the only mediums that remained were those of word of mouth, flyers, and posters. These methods Apollos employed, and before long, interested, potential students began to stop in and see what the new school had to offer. In all, from the day he first identified the location to the day NATAC had its official grand opening to enroll students for its first class took the determined Ihedigbos a total of six months.

When NATAC finally opened its doors, it was only one of a few places to gain computer training in Umuahia. Computer technology training was simply not accessible in the primary schools run by Nigeria's educational system. In fact, most Nigerian students then and today will graduate from high school with very limited knowledge of computer technology.

Apollos and Rose had to keep these things in mind when shaping the programs and pricing structure of NATAC. They knew that there were many school dropouts who decided to leave school for a variety of reasons usually because their parents could no longer afford to send them to school. Most elementary and middle schools in Nigeria are government run and are free; however, education beyond this point usually requires financing that many Nigerians simply do not have. Therefore, NATAC's programs were designed to be affordable, and if a family was struggling to pay tuition, the school's administrators would work out flexible payment options for them to attend, even offering a limited number of scholarships.

Then they knew that those of lower incomes could not afford to go to college, so they ensured that this population would be able to afford NATAC's computer training programs, which upon completion could offer them access to a good job with good pay, leading to a good life.

Next, NATAC would help to provide solutions to struggles that the people of Umuahia experienced with their education systems in general. To put it lightly, the Nigerian educational system is lacking when compared with the rest of the world. There are very few books and materials in the government-run schools, and the resources that are available for the instruction of students are often outdated. As a result, children who graduate from these schools are not equipped to succeed in life, having not been adequately prepared with the educational essentials necessary to gain admission to local universities where they can further their education. Often, only those children whose parents are able to send them to private schools that offer a higher quality of educational training are prepared with the necessary skills to pass entrance tests and gain admission to a university. In light of this, Apollos and Rose structured NATAC's programs to provide affordable remedial courses for graduates of government schools that would prepare these students with the essentials necessary to qualify for a spot at a four-year university.

The people of Umuahia knew that NATAC was owned by Americans, and they were accustomed to schools of this sort opening up in their city. However, there was no special preference granted to the new school by the general public—NATAC would have to prove itself through its programming and quality of professionalism just like all of the other schools of its kind that existed. Apollos and Rose would ensure that their countrymen were not disappointed by the new institution that would soon capture local attention and become a permanent fixture in the Umuahia community.

From the vantage point of onlookers who lived ordinary lives, it appeared as though the Ihedigbos were accomplishing monumental things that most people would consider utterly impossible.

"Since I was around a lot, I would often hear Apollos and Rose talk about the school they wanted to start in Nigeria," Esther, a close family friend explains. "Pretty much from nothing, they started the school. They started seeking and receiving donations, and when I finally realized the depth of what they were doing, I was amazed. They were sending shipping containers the size of railroad train cars full of things that they had gotten donated from people to Nigeria—hundreds and hundreds of computers, clothes, medications, books, you name it! And all because they had made a commitment to come to America, improve their lives, and go back and uplift their people. Then they would travel back and forth from Massachusetts to Nigeria to work on the school, and before long, they had graduated students. Just like that! It was an absolutely remarkable thing to witness from start to finish. My two friends, ordinary people in all regards, but doing extraordinary things."

At the same time that Apollos was in Nigeria, progressing his vision of NATAC as a single soldier, his daughter, Onyii, was stuck in advancing a vision of her own. She'd recently completed a marketing fellowship at the Arena Stage in Washington, D.C., a renowned theater company, but she didn't know what she wanted to do next. She knew that she didn't want a corporate job; in fact, she'd been offered a good one but declined it without hesitation because she didn't want to settle—she wanted to figure things out for her next big step in life. Deep inside, she knew what she'd really wanted to do—she wanted to be in Africa; however, she had no idea of what vehicle or means would get here there. Onyii was on a journey to discover what she would become.

No sooner than Onyii began her journey did her father contact her from Nigeria. As she expressed over the phone how much she wanted to be there with him to help him with the school, Apollos encouraged her to apply for a program that he thought would be good for her: the International Foundation for Education and Self-help (IFESH) program based in Arizona. Though she was unfamiliar with this program at the time, her father explained that the program paid students to work in Africa. He knew that Africa was where she, his eldest child, desired to be, even when she desperately replied, "I don't want to just be in *Africa*. I want to be in *Nigeria*—with you!"

To this, Apollos, ever the wise one in touch with the Spirit, smiling to himself on the other end, simply answered, "Maybe they will place you right here."

Onyii proceeded to apply for participation in the IFESH program and learned that competition in the United States was stiff—they would only choose fewer than fifty people to participate. Soon after, she received the letter she'd been waiting for that informed her of the news: she had been selected as a standby. If one of the individuals selected for the program declined the offer to travel to Africa, she would be next in line. Working as He does, the Lord's purpose prevailed. As soon as the first person declined the offer, Onyii was selected to travel and was positioned to work with an NGO (non-governmental organization) in Zimbabwe.

Upon receipt of the news, Onyii called her father to notify him of the latest advancement.

"Daddy, I got accepted, but I'm not coming to Nigeria, I'm going to Zimbabwe. I really wanted to come to be in Nigeria with you!" she cried to her father, defeated.

Apollos' response was simple. "The Lord will provide," he said with the spiritual confidence that marked his life.

Immediately, Onyii traveled to her required training at the IFESH headquarters in Arizona, and two quick weeks later, she departed for Zimbabwe. The NGO to which she was assigned involved working with one of the country's elected officials, Mavis Chizanga. Not long after her arrival, however, IFESH informed Onyii that the program was not being operated according to specifications surrounding the assignments of workers and she would have to be transferred to another program, this time in South Africa. Seizing the opportunity, Rose and Apollos's eldest asked to go to Nigeria to work with her father. IFESH agreed and paid for everything. Twelve weeks after she had arrived in Zimbabwe, a grateful Onyii Ihedigbo arrived in Nigeria.

Apollos had been working in Nigeria for seven months prior to his daughter's arrival and knew that she had been sent to serve with him for such a time as this. As Onyii greeted her father at the airport, she was filled with love and adoration for the larger-than-life gentle giant that had groomed her for so many years in strength, spirituality, education, and passion for helping others. However, Onyii, a keen observer of her father for many years, immediately knew that something was wrong. Watching him closely, she noticed that he was exhibiting symptoms of memory loss—the giant was weakening, and this broke her heart.

Upon seeing his daughter arrive in West Africa's Port Harcourt, Apollos openly sobbed for joy. Since he'd arrived in Nigeria by himself, he'd felt so alone and lonely for his family back in the U.S., particularly the love of his life, the one knitted so closely to his heart that she was a part of its fabric—Rose. Aside from the time that he was without her soon after they were married and he'd departed alone from Nigeria for Houghton College, he had never really been without her. Now it had been about two years since he had experienced her loving embrace, and it showed all over his face and throughout his disposition. To Onyii, seeing her father broken like this was intensely sad—very difficult to watch—and she was more sure than ever that the Lord had delivered her, through His divine providence, to be there with her father and help him with his work.

When Apollos went to Nigeria to establish NATAC, much of the time, he stayed in his home village. This might seem odd—an accomplished Nigerian-American who was considered by most standards very prosperous choosing to stay in the dusty rural village of his childhood. This village, which lacked electricity and hot running water, was a far cry from the comforts of his home in the U.S., and it was also a far cry from the amenities very nice semi luxury hotels that were only a thirty-minute drive from the quaint, familiar village in which he chose to say.

There could be many explanations as to why Apollos chose to stay in the village, but they always boiled down to the fact that the village is where his family was—and Apollos loved his family. Especially with his wife and children miles away in Massachusetts, he felt the need to be around those of the same blood in a comfortable and easy atmosphere that accepted him equally for what he was and what he was not. The village represented family, familiarity, and home.

However true this explanation may be, Onyii, who eventually went to live with her father in Nigeria as he did his work, has a different viewpoint.

"The reason my dad stayed in the village, I think," she explains, "is that he suffered from a guilt of 'I made it and I succeeded and got out of the village,' so he felt an obligation to stay there and show that no matter what he accomplished, he was no greater—he was trying to show that he was still one of them and always would be."

Though life was not always easy for Apollos in the village, he endured and would not leave; there was too much work to be done for the people in his village for him to do so. No matter what comfort, convenience, or security it cost him, he would remain in the village.

Once, when asked why he stayed in the village and cared about the people in it so much, he replied, "I made a promise to God. The reason He let me leave was so that I could give back." This sentiment serves as the perfect summary of Apollos's entire life's work, giving his life to establish a better life for others in Nigeria.

The work that stood before Apollos to establish a school for his people was a formidable one, but with Christ, he believed, all things were possible. Waking early to launch into the great feat before him, he would make the necessary visits throughout the regions to gain the proper permitting, licensures, and documents that would qualify his school as an official entity operating in Nigeria. Through the loud static of the international phone lines, he would fight to understand the brokers and product suppliers on the other end, arranging for books, computer equipment, medical supplies, and other vital resources to be shipped in the nearly seven thousand miles across the Atlantic Ocean to arrive at Port Harcourt. These activities not only cost the aging gentleman a lot of money but time, and he exhausted as much mental energy as physical energy in the pursuit of his goals on a daily basis.

Since 1995, Transparency International has published the Corruption Perceptions Index, an annual ranking of how countries fare in their levels of corruption according to expert assessments and opinion surveys. Countries are ranked on a scale from 1 to 10, with 10 suggesting that a society experiences very little to no corruption and 1 suggesting full-blown, pervasive corruption. During the time of Apollos's work in Nigeria, the country never broke a two—and based on the amount of energy he had to exert to get things done, he was a firsthand witness to this. Trying to accomplish good things for people in a corrupt context has a way of making even the most pure-hearted of men with the most noble of intentions falter in his ability to believe in the general goodness of man.

One such incident came after Apollos had coordinated, paid for, and shipped two containers from the United States to Nigeria, one containing books and the other containing medical equipment. Onyii, who was working in Nigeria with her father at the time, describes the ordeal that surrounded the release of the containers.

"The containers with the books arrived at Port Harcourt, and they notified us that it was there, but it was 'held up.' In order to have them released, my dad called a broker to come to the house, someone who said he knew the officials and the systems and guaranteed the release of the books. My dad believed him and handed over a large African striped bag full of naira. Cash money. Soon the container with the books was delivered to our school, and although we had to jump through so many hoops to get the books, we were very happy," Onyii explains.

The success that Apollos enjoyed with the broker negotiating the release of his books was unfortunately not long lived. After spending thousands of dollars on a container filled to the brim with medical equipment, this container too found itself held captive by the port's officials.

"My cousin Amara and I were in Nigeria at the same time that we were trying to get this container released. We decided that we were going to act as the undercover American detectives about to blow the roof off this operation. We didn't care about how much trouble we might get in as the 'crazy Americans.' Every time my dad went to the port authorities to try to negotiate the release of his container, we went with him, secretly carrying tape recorders hidden in our lapels. When one of the officials would say something denying my father the release of his equipment, leaning deliberately forward, we would ask, 'Kwuo ya ozo?' which means 'Say it again?' in Igbo. My dad never knew that we were recording them as they shifted us from department to department and gave excuse after excuse."

In another desperate attempt to get his hands on his valued possessions, Apollos called his broker, hoping for another miracle—one that never came, according to Onyii.

"The broker came over to the house and got the money to get the container released, but this time, the container was not delivered. Two weeks later, the guy came back and said, 'They want more money.' My dad was so trusting of people that he never believed they would take advantage of him, he also didn't believe that God would allow it to be so. This broker, whom he only barely knew, he fully trusted. He gave the man more than one hundred thousand U.S. dollars to get the container out and sent him on his way. Any other person would have sent security with him or at least followed him!"

Apollos and Onyii never saw the container filled with medical equipment that he had so painstakingly worked to bring to his homeland.

"As scarce as resources were, and as much as my father had paid for the equipment, the shipping, and everything else, that loss was a heartbreaking one. My dad had even sold the land in Port Harcourt that we'd planned to build a house on for our family, just so he could have things for our school. All they saw was the American cash, and they went for it."

Though they never saw their container of medical equipment, ironically, they did see the same broker driving himself around in a yellow brand-new Mercedes Benz soon after they had released their monies to him. Such situations commonly comprised the tales of those trying to forge ahead to build better lives for others in Nigeria.

While Apollos might appear to have become more gullible and trusting in Nigeria from his daughter's point of view, his spiritual keenness seemed to be as sharp as ever. He could still hear the voice of the Holy Spirit as clearly as ever, and he demonstrated this to his daughter in an amazing account that still confounds her mind to this day.

"Onyii!" Apollos called out. "Wake up, Onyii! Your cousin Amara is coming. She's on her way!"

Onyii begrudgingly turned over under the covers of the soft, warm bed, eyes squinting at the bright African sunlight that shone through the window. Her initial reaction was one of great joy, as Amara was one of her dearest cousins and had shared many experiences with her growing up. However, in an instant, she shook off her grogginess and, with a clear mind replied, "Daddy, you are crazy! Amara is in America, remember?"

Unswayed by his daughter's response, Apollos confidently responded, "God told me Amara is coming. I did not say Amara was coming *here*. Of course, she would have to go to Lagos first, and then she would have to go to Aba. So let's go to Aba!" he said with a big, cheerful grin.

Not quite understanding what was going on, Onyii reluctantly rolled out of the bed and dressed herself. After sharing breakfast with her father, the two ventured out of the door and boarded the public transport to Aba. As they rode along in the tiny beat-up minivan that provided public transportation to the citizens of the region, Onyii remained confused yet watchful. She had never known her father's spiritual impulses to be off, for he was a spiritually keen man, very attuned to the Spirit's voice and the Father's leading. Bouncing around along the rough terrain of unpaved roads as dust surrounded the loud little vehicle desperately in need of a tune-up, she periodically glanced at her father's face. He was as happy and content as ever, and his eyes shined brightly as he braced himself for the van's bouts with the potholes in the road. It was clear that he was looking forward to seeing his niece Amara any moment now.

"You stop praying, girl! Stop praying and cover your head!"

Onyii was startled by the cries of the older women that surrounded her in the little van. In Nigeria, when one is on the transport, it is commonplace to pray constantly. These prayers, offered by both men and women, are against the demon of the road, and the entreaties towards God are that He would not allow this road demon to come that day and take the sacrifice of their lives. However, many religious denominations abound in Nigeria, each with its own list of traditions, restrictions, and requirements; one such requirement is the covering of the head when praying against the road demon. Without a word, one of the older women reached into her gritty knapsack, pulled out an old, unseemly rag, and placed it atop of Onyii's head. That was also the day that Onyii learned to carry her own handkerchief.

"We'll get off ahead in the Aba town center," Apollos said as he nudged Onyii. "The Spirit told me to go this way."

"This guy's crazy," Onyii muttered to herself as they edged their way through the crowd to step out of the small van, which sped off leaving them standing in a small cloud of dust and exhaust. Nonetheless, she followed her father.

"I know you don't believe me," he said, sensing his daughter's clear doubt. He continued to walk, his daughter curiously following close behind, providing commentary on every turn along the path with, "The Spirit told me to turn here. The Spirit told me to go this way." After a variety of twists and turns on and off the road, Apollos proudly announced, "The Holy Spirit says go right here! Right here!"

There they stood on the side of the street—in silence. As much as she wanted to, Onyii restrained herself from saying, "I thought you said the Holy Spirit was leading you to Amara. I don't see her here, so what now?" Instead, she stood silently by the side of her father, looking around for something she knew was not present for the sake of honoring her father. How could she help her father save face in this situation? Perhaps she would give her father a few minutes then suggest that they hop on the next public transport van that pulled up and make the ride back to their home, never to bring the story up again.

Two minutes later, Onyii saw a van headed their way. By the time she built up enough confidence to nudge her father with the unspoken suggestion that perhaps they should get on it, the van stopped directly in front of them—and Amara stepped out.

"Uncle Apollos!" Amara screamed with tone that mixed sheer delight and disbelief all at once. "Uncle! Onyii! What are you *doing* here?" As her excited cousin jumped towards her for a big hug and did the same for her uncle, Onyii stood clearly fazed and stunned.

"I cannot believe you are here! Oh my God, this cannot be real! I cannot *believe* it!" Amara squealed.

"You didn't *know* we would be here?" Onyii finally asked once she was able to speak.

"No! I told no one! I didn't even know how I would be able to find you once I got here from America," Amara said, still jumping with glee.

"Didn't I tell you?" Apollos said, glancing down at his daughter with a knowing smile, though not a smug one. Onyii would never doubt her father's spiritual leading again.

Not only did Onyii recognize her father Apollos as the spiritual giant he was, but the people of his village recognized and respected him as such too. Each time Apollos would return back to his village from the U.S., he would bring mounds and mounds of clothes for the men and women and boys and girls. Hearing Apollos's car drive into the village on the bumpy dirt road, his family members would run outside to witness his arrival and perhaps sneak a peek at the number of boxes of goodies he brought along with him this time from the States.

Before the car could even come to a full stop, it was surrounded by nieces, nephews, brothers, sisters, aunts, and uncles shouting, "*Dédè!* Uncle! Do you have anything for me? Do you have anything for me? Where is my Christmas?" they would ask expectantly. Without a doubt, Apollos had something for everyone in his village, and returning home with such practical goodies made him feel special; that the Lord used him to bless so many people in his village gave him a sense of joy and fulfillment like nothing else could.

Box by box, Apollos would bring the clothes and household goods to his brother's house to distribute them to his family members. Sometimes, he would even pile them on top of his mother's grave that sat at the center of the compound and ration them out. Before long, however, the people of the village had had enough of the clothes—they wanted money. It was at this time that Apollos began to encounter many break-ins into his village home with thieves repeatedly stealing his cash and belongings. In fact, whenever Apollos left, those watching him used it as an opportunity to violate his home once again, stealing money from the accomplished man they perceived to be the wealthy American.

It was clear that the continual break-ins of Apollos's home within the village were an inside job; more specifically, it was his cousin. One time, Apollos, who was known to speak things and they would be so, had had enough.

Returning home to find his home burglarized once again, he stepped outside into the compound and asked with a strong yet controlled anger, "Who took the money?" No one answered.

"Where is the money?" he demanded again strongly in his thick Igbo accent, looking around the compound at people who clearly knew the answer but refused to point out one of their own. Still, no one spoke a word.

"Well then," he started, "I declare this day that whoever took that money shall die by that money!"

Instantly, his audience at the center of the compound cried, "No, Uncle! Please! Uncle, please! Please take it back! Don't say that they will die! Uncle, please! We can find who took this money! Please!" they pleaded with Apollos. However, he was firm and resolute in his declaration, and he would not withdraw it. He was God's man in the Spirit, and when he spoke it, he knew that it would come to pass.

A few weeks later, one of the poor cousins from the village who had never before had the resources to purchase anything of significance rolled into the compound with a brand-new motorcycle—to an audience of odd and awkward stares.

"Where did you get the money to buy a motorcycle, and such a nice one?" they asked cautiously.

"Oh, I was doing business and business has been good," he replied elusively as he proudly flaunted his new bike. Two weeks later, this cousin was dead—he died in an accident when his motorcycle was hit by another.

The people of the village believed in the power of the spoken word, especially when it was spoken by a man as powerful and spiritually attuned as Apollos Ihedigbo. He was one of God's true representatives, especially out of his office as a pastor. As a result, when Apollos spoke, people listened.

Despite incidents such as these, Apollos remained dedicated to his village, contently living in his village home amidst his own people. Each time he was violated, he forgave the violator, asking God to forgive them "for they know not what they do." With the strongest level of compassion possible, the spiritual giant never gave up on the idea that people were generally good and that they could change, that he could actually help make the people better. Even when taken advantage of, he would simply reply, "My life is not my own."

By maintaining such a strong kingdom disposition in the midst of his trials, Apollos brought more back to his village than he would ever realize. Yes, he brought clothing and household goods, and yes, he brought money, but above all things, he brought to life what a living, breathing, loving, forgiving, functioning example of what a Christian life lived out before the Lord looked like. Even when he knew he was being taken advantage of, he was willing to give anything and everything, even sacrificing himself. People could look to him and live, and outside of Christ Himself, this example was the greatest gift for which the village could ever hope.

Other than the challenges of daily grind and the typical economic, social, and political obstacles that test the will and characterize typical Nigerian life, Onyii and Apollos relished the time they spent together in their home country while working on NATAC. Perhaps the most consistent challenge that they faced in Nigeria was that of the police checkpoints that litter the landscape, checkpoints that serve no real official purpose other than to shake down the travelers that they detain for money. Apollos and Onyii had been stopped many times by the police.

Slam! Slam! Slam! Onyii was not startled as she rolled slowly through the police checkpoint, and the waiting policeman who stood at the checkpoint banged on the top of her Volvo with a flat, open hand. In the other hand, he carried an AK-47 machine gun.

"Why are you stopping us?" Onyii asked excitedly, clearly perturbed at the constant harassment she and her father had repeatedly endured at the hands of the officers. Today, however, her father was not with her, but her cousin Amara was. The officer said nothing, only made the motion for her to pull the car over.

"I'm not pulling over! Why are you stopping me?" she asked again in her loud, strong Nigerian accent that always emerged when she grew incredibly passionate about something. Amara looked at her cousin as if she was crazy. In reality, Onyii was simply fed up.

The officer finally spoke as he leaned in to the Volvo's open window. "What are you going to give me?" he asked, conspicuously handling his gun to add further intimidation.

At this, Onyii unloaded on the officer. "You should be ashamed of yourself!" she yelled loudly out the window in her thick Igbo accent. Onyii had always been a handful. A fireball. A very strong-minded, strong-willed type of girl who was unafraid to stand up to anyone or anything. This was a fact to which her brothers would easily attest.

"Who are you?" he sternly demanded in a bold, strong voice, unaccustomed to such resistance.

"I am your *sisterrrrr*!" she shouted, drawing out the last word for stronger effect. "And you should be ashamed of yourself for treating me this way! Are you going to shoot an American citizen? What type of news would that be in Nigeria? You should be ashamed that you are doing this to your own people!" she screamed. With that, Onyii sped away in the Volvo, leaving the very embarrassed officer behind in a cloud of dust at the checkpoint.

Onyii acknowledges her unusually strong sense of boldness in that encounter. "Not many women would even drive in Nigeria, but I needed to get around, so I just got in the car and started going. That was *very* American of me!" she says with a giggle.

Throughout her time working in Nigeria with her father, not everything was all business all the time. At one point, she fell head over heels in "like" with a talented poet named Jonas; however, he was from her village, and such relationships from people of the same village were culturally forbidden due to the inevitability of their being related in some way. In any case, despite this culturally-forbidden taboo, she relished her time with this dreamy, creative, intellectual, a soft-spoken Nigerian man.

"Every day he would write me a poem," she explains. "He was so smart, and he knew so much. He studied philosophy, he was knowledgeable about the arts, and it seemed he'd read *everything*! He could have easily been a professor at a university, but he was so young at the time. We would sneak off into the village to see each other just so we could chill and talk. I really fell for him, but my cousins were like, 'You know he is your *brother*. You can't talk to him, Onyii, he is your *brother*!' It caused such an uproar in the village that we had to cut it off. We didn't know exactly how we were related, but if you're from the same village, you had to be related some kind of way."

Over time, in the midst of the daily challenges they faced in working with the school, Onyii began to see her father's health deteriorate even further than when he'd first greeted her at the airport as she arrived from Zimbabwe. She explains the process of watching her father's symptoms become more and more pronounced.

"When I got there from Zimbabwe, my mom sent my dad money, which we took to the bank. After spending about a week in the village, he said he didn't have any money at all. He had all of this money in the bank, but he wouldn't remember going to deposit it—he'd completely forgotten about it. His mind was worsening right before my very eyes."

On another occasion, Rose and the Ihedigbo boys came to Nigeria for a visit, and Apollos was elated. The family shared very special time together for the holiday, but as with all trips, the good time had to come to an end. Apollos and Onyii took Rose and the boys to the bus station and said their good-byes, and once they boarded the bus and pulled off into the distance, Apollos and Onyii returned home and went to bed for the evening. However, in the middle of the night, Apollos awoke and asked for his wife in a panic.

"Dad, we dropped her off at the bus station with the boys earlier. Don't you remember?" she asked. All her poor father could do was cry.

Part of what concerned the family the most was the level of vulnerability to being taken advantage of that Apollos now found himself in as a result of his declining health. Not only did he forget small things like where he'd bought his soda bottles so that he could return them to the right factory to get his deposit back, he would forget essential things like who he'd given money to and whether he'd gotten it back. Unfortunately, these challenges with his memory cost him hundreds of thousands of lost U.S. dollars.

As a result, his daughter began to journal his days and watch everywhere he went very closely.

After seven months of working with her father in Nigeria, it was time for Onyii to return to the U.S. This was perhaps one of the most difficult decisions she'd ever had to make in her life, as she knew that her father was not in any condition to be left alone. Even prior to her leaving, she had to drive to Port Harcourt to point out several men to the authorities who had taken advantage of her father, make sure they were arrested, and then ensure that they were charged and put in jail before her departure. Nonetheless, Onyii departed a plane and headed back for the United States with hopes of returning someday soon to Nigeria to pick up where she'd left off.

Again without his daughter, Apollos continued the work of NATAC. Unfortunately, only two years after he opened the school, he faced an untimely demise. Dr. Apollos Ihedigbo passed away on January 7, 2002. Before he closed his eyes on earth, however, the Lord blessed him to see his vision come to pass.

The vision of NATAC still continues today.

THE UNFORGETTABLE LEGACY OF APOLLOS NDULAKA (LIFE WILL TELL) IHEDIGBO

Apollos Ihedigbo loved his children as much as it is possible for a father to love his genetic offspring—living, walking, breathing mirror images of oneself that make a man's heart burst with pride and humility. He recognized that he was an example to a unique group of youth and that they were watching his every move. Rather than shirk this responsibility as too many Western fathers choose to do or leave the responsibility of training of his children to the media to passively groom them towards secularity, Apollos lived up to the responsibility on every occasion. "I must be an example for my children, or someone else would be," he thought. He would be not just a man, but a godly man with a passion for the Lord that would impart spiritual and practical wisdom into their lives while he had the chance. "No one knows how long I will be with you, so always remember what I taught you," he would say.

The relationship that this dad had with his children, though not a perfect one—as such do not exist—was a very close and committed one. "It touched my heart to see Apollos with his boys. He would grab them in a big hug and shower them with kisses as they tried to pull away. He was very affectionate," recounts family friend Esther, a frequent guest of the household. "To me, he came across as a stern but lighthearted father. He clowned around with the kids all the time, grabbing them and shaking them around a little bit. Or they would come behind him and playfully grab him from behind until he got his bearings, and then he would find a way to flip the script and shake or tickle them until they collapsed in giggles and begged for mercy!"

"My dad showed his love through lots of affection, and he played with us a lot," recalls James. "There was this game that he used to do with us whether at church or at his office. If you ever shook his hand, he would start laughing and say, 'Oh, you're trying to test my strength, huh?' And then he would squeeze your knuckles together until you were on your knees, squealing, 'Okay, I give up! I give up!' Once he got you to give up the test of his strength, he would just laugh and laugh. He loved to play."

Some of the Ihedigbos' fondest memories happened in the car. Embarking on a journey to their chosen destination, whether it was down the street to the grocery store or to another state for an African Christian Fellowship event, the clan loved to ride together in the close confines of the family car. This was one of the settings where they felt like the close-knit group they were; it helped to reinforce part of their identity as they went where they went as one unit—a family that was securely strapped in with Dad at the helm of the boat. They rode along with love and simplicity of heart, thanking God for the little things that made such a big impact on their lives.

Occasionally, the peaceful car ride would take a turn. Emeka might have said something to Nate, Nate might have poked James, and in their scuffling, they accidently hit their sister, Onyii, while David simply shook his head at the sight, and then the bickering would begin! However, Dad was masterful in diffusing conflict which is inevitable in a family of seven riding along in a station wagon. In the midst of the chaos that was occurring in the backseats behind him, he would make a funny joke, and everyone in the car would crack up laughing. He knew how to manage his brood, not with a heavy hand, but with love.

If there is one of the Ihedigbo sons that could lay claim to being Apollos's best friend in the family, it would be David; though he had many friends his own age, he loved that fact that he and his father were best friends. David was the son that never said no to his father. As soon as Apollos would say, "Come play tennis,"

David would pick up his racket and lace up his shoes. As soon as Apollos would say, "I need you to take me to the mall," David would grab his wallet and his keys. He enjoyed every moment with his father, from assembling things they'd purchased and fixing things that were broken and even when attending auctions together, something Apollos loved to do. David considered himself closest to his father because he was the one who was always around him.

Though he adored his son David, Apollos was full of a father's wisdom and took every opportunity he could to disseminate it every one of the children who were the fruit of his loins—especially when he had a captive audience. During these times, he would share stories of his upbringing, how he'd overcome challenge and adversity to reach a goal of accomplishing a task, and during these times, his children would listen. For example, when the children missed the school bus, which happened far too often in Apollos's estimation, he would drive them to school, but the trip was made a little longer in the children's minds by the endless stories he would tell.

"How could you miss the bus?" he would ask, choosing to use his thick Nigerian accent for such rebukes. "All you have to do is wake up on time, put on your clothes, and walk outside. You kids take too many things for granted! In Nigeria, I used to have to walk two miles to school with books in hand, and yet you're too lazy to wake up and take a bus that will drive you to where you are going!" As tedious as they thought their father's stories were, eyes rolling as they rode along listening from the back seat, the stories took. Little did they know, one day, it would be these very stories that they would reflect upon in their own lives to inspire them towards attaining their own goals.

There are rare times when we see war generals at vulnerable points in their lives, and nothing is more painful. These stalwart commanders, responsible for ensuring that a group of individuals under their charge, take great pride in keeping their troops healthy and alive; strategizing for their care and providing for their needs are priority for these men who would lay down their very lives for those under their care. However, there are times when we see these generals, these great men, falter; if we watch closely, at times that occur as infrequently as a solar eclipse, we see them at great points of weakness and vulnerability. During these rare times, few things in life are more difficult to witness than seeing the strongest man in your life fail to deliver for his troops, and you see on his face the realization that he has made such an epic failure, his disappointment in himself palpable. The youngest Ihedigbo, James, vividly recalls seeing his father in such a rare moment.

"When we lived on Tamarack Drive, one time, my dad forgot to pay the electric bill, so the power was out. Because she could not cook without power, my mom went to Burger King and got a bunch of Whoppers for us. We lit candles throughout the house and sat down to eat. I remember sitting next to my dad, who didn't have a burger, and asked him if he was going to eat. He said no because he was so upset. Taking care of his family was priority to him, and falling short was huge for him. He couldn't believe he had fallen short like this. It never, ever, ever happened again."

Ask family friends and loved ones about their fondest memory of Dr. Apollos Ihedigbo, and the answer is always unanimous: pizza night at the Ihedigbo house. The hospitable African gentleman was notorious for saying, "Hey, come on over to the house on Friday night for pizza!"

"The first time," a family friend recalls, "I thought we were going to order pizza. But as soon as I walked in, there Apollos was in the kitchen with sleeves rolled up and a big grin, several big balls of pizza dough from Antonio's Pizza in front of him, surrounded by happy family and friends who could not wait to watch him make his famous pizza." Apollos would masterfully fashion the balls of white and whole wheat dough, topping them with a spread of ingredients that included the finest pepperoni, chicken, and any other preferred meats and veggies. He relished this time when his hungry audience would watch with big smiles and mouths watering as their father and friend made the best pizza, not only in Massachusetts, but in the whole world!

Every one of the children had a job to do on pizza night. As soon as Apollos walked through the door with the dough, it was all hands on deck, and everyone was excited to play a part—though not necessarily the part to which they were assigned. James's job was always to grate the cheese for six or seven pizzas, a task that could take an uncomfortable toll on small elbows. "Dad," he would plead, "this is a lot! Why don't you just buy the cheese that's already grated?" To this, his father would reply with good-natured smile, "No! The block cheese is cheaper, so keep grating!"

Sitting around the table, Apollos and his crew ate the fresh, cheesy pizzas as they came piping hot out of the oven, laughing, joking, ribbing one another, and telling stories of faith, stories of hardship in Nigeria, and wisdom-filled life lessons that would carry the Ihedigbo children down the road to success. Pizza time was family time.

After the pizza pans had been picked clean of all of their extra cheese and toppings and the table was cleared, David's favorite part of the evening was the time of fellowship that he would spend around the television as he, his brothers, their closest cousins, and their family friends played video games on the Atari. As soon as they were excused from the table, off the boys would run to continue the competition they had begun before the fresh pizza came out of the oven. Nate and Emeka would always go first because they were older, and this was just their rule: "We're older, so we're going to go first!" David, James, and the rest of the boys they had over for company would sit patiently on the sofa, awaiting their turn to the controller and cheering the best player on and cracking jokes against the player who allowed his opponent to score too easily.

The children loved these times of fellowship with one another, especially with their fellow Nigerians. It was loud—very loud—and even a bit chaotic, as each of the boys tried to remember whose turn it would be next in the rotation to play the winner at Techno Bowl, and when the jokes about one another started flying, causing side-splitting laughter among the boys, it got even louder.

Upstairs was no different, however, because it was equally loud if not louder. Here in the living room, Apollos and Rose would be talking with the other adults. Inevitably, their conversations would always seem to turn serious, and when Nigerians get serious, they get loud!

"Hearing the commotion, I always used to come upstairs to ask my dad and my uncle, 'Why are you arguing?' Whenever we got together, they would get so loud and intense, going back and forth in their Igbo accents that I thought they were going to fight each other! They would take a temporary pause and calmly say, 'David, we are not fighting, we are just talking loudly.' It always turned out to be the same old things that drove them to this point—confusion over what really happened in a story they both tried to tell, competitions, and someone always wanting to be right. Eventually, my mom would say, 'Stop it! Quiet down!' and things would get back to normal. An onlooker might think it was too dramatic an environment to have a good time, but it was all in good Nigerian fun." The family took great pleasure in these times of letting loose and having fun with their father.

And then it happened.

Just after Onyii's wedding in December 2001, Apollos, who had flown in from Nigeria to attend the wedding, seemed to look a bit out of it. David asked his father if everything was okay, and Apollos replied that he was fine. Though Rose and David tried to convince him to stay until New Year's, he explained that he simply had too much work to do, so it was imperative that he immediately return to Nigeria.

Before his departure, however, he sat his son David down and had a serious talk.

"When my dad sat me down," David explains, "he said, 'I want you to watch over our family and keep track of your mom. Right now, your mom has four husbands here. I want *you* to keep watch over your mom.' Even to this day, I looked at it as my dad saying he was going to pass away soon, and he left me with the one responsibility to keep this family together. He said it over and over again, almost like he was giving me ownership to continue the legacy that he had established by watching over the family."

Not long after his father's return to Nigeria, the Ihedigbo house phone rang. Only Rose, David, and James lived in the house now, and since David was awake, he answered.

"Hello? Hi, it's your cousin from Nigeria. Who's this?" the caller asked.

"It's David. What's up?" he inquired, knowing that any call from Nigeria had to be important. It was morning in Massachusetts, and Nigeria was six hours ahead of them. Perhaps they had been waiting until they were sure the family was awake to make the call.

"I am calling to tell you that your father Apollos has fallen ill. He is in the hospital, and he is not doing well. We must speak to your mother. Is she there?" Concerned but not overly so, David went to his mother's bedroom and asked her to pick up the phone.

After a few minutes, Rose emerged and came back with a report for David. "Your father is sick, but I spoke with him and he said he is okay. I'm going to have to get a ticket and go out there."

The next day, the family received another phone call notifying them that Apollos had taken a turn for the worse. In haste, the congregation of the Ihedigbos' church pooled their money together to send their sister Rose to be at the side of her ailing husband in Nigeria. While she was in flight, David got yet another phone call letting them know that his father had taken a turn for the better. Looking back, David had always thought that receiving these two phone calls with different reports of his father's health was odd.

Before her plane departed to carry her to her sick husband, Rose called Apollos's dear friend, Dr. Okorafor, with whom he'd graduated from UMass.

"Brother Daniel…" she mumbled, "I am…leaving to go… to Nigeria. I must…see about…the situation with Apollos." Dr. Okorafor and his wife, whom he had called over to the phone, could barely understand what their friend was saying. She mumbled through her words because she didn't even have the strength to speak clearly.

"Are you okay, Sister Rose? Do you have everything you need?" he asked, concerned about his friend.

"Yes…yes. The church collected money…I am going…" she drifted off. If he had been standing before her, he knew that Rose would have looked as numb as she sounded.

After saying their good-byes and assuring their friend that they would be in prayer for her and Apollos, Daniel and Evelyn Okorafor began to pray, not only for the healing of Apollos, but for the sustenance of Rose, a strong, mighty woman whom they'd never seen falter in such a way.

As soon as she landed in Nigeria on January 6, at three o'clock in the afternoon, Rose went straight to the hospital not sure of what to expect. In Nigeria, if someone is sick at the hospital, the family member of the patient had to go out and purchase the medicine for the doctors to use. Most major ailments are ones that can be easily treated if the family has the proper resources. She hoped she wasn't too late.

As she anxiously rushed into the area of the hospital where her husband lay in bed, she was pleasantly surprised at what she saw. Apollos was leading prayers and singing songs with all of the rest of the patients. As she stepped through the door, his face lit up.

"Enyi, you're here!" he said happily with a weakened voice.

Working with the physicians, Rose immediately coordinated the transfer of her husband to another hospital at which it was believed he could receive better help. Later that same evening, as his friend and beloved wife sat at his bedside, at 4:00 a.m. Apollos Ndulaka Ihedigbo closed his eyes for the last time and departed from this life—but not before uttering his final words: "God is not finished with us!"

"It was almost like he was fighting and fighting, holding on just so he could see my mother one last time," David says of his father's passing. "When she got there, it was his release—like saying 'It's my time to go.'" His father's last four words are permanently inked on David's left arm today.

"It was senior year in high school," recalls James. "I was in science class. I remember my teacher getting a call from the principal's office. After she hung up, she said, 'Mr. Ihedigbo, you need to go to the principal's office now.' As I slowly organized my things, I thought of all of the reasons I might be called in to the office. I was a senior, after all, so there might have been reasons for me to be summonsed to the office, but I hadn't skipped class, parked in the teacher's lot, or been late for class this week. When I got to the principal's office, my mom's best friend, Esther, was waiting there for me, sitting there with the principal. *What is she doing here?* I thought. I walked in to the open door to the office, and the principal walked out of the office, leaving us alone.

"Esther turned to me and said, 'We have to go home.' 'Why?' I asked. 'I'm sorry, but your father passed away,' she answered solemnly. I know that Esther drove me home, but my mind doesn't even remember the car ride home. I just remember getting into her van, sitting in the back passenger seat, and closing the door. Everything else was blank after that. I checked out. There was no sound, kind of like when you're watching a scene in a movie when you see people talking and crying, but it's completely silent because the sound is gone. Everything was on mute. I was just trying to process the information.

"I remember thinking, *Yeah, right. No, he didn't. There's no way my dad passed away*. I thought this all the way home until we arrived at the house on Bedford Court. At the time, only me, my mom, and my brother David were living there. When I got home, all of my brothers were already there along with some people from the church, and everyone was crying. I remember my mom calling me all the way from Nigeria because she was worried about how I was doing. Out of all of my siblings, she called me. She was worried about me. It was one of those things that would take a long time to settle in. My dad was really gone."

❧

Emeka stood in front of the restaurant bar that he managed in Amherst, Massachusetts. As the assistant general manager, it was his job to make sure that his regular guests were cared for, so there he stood, cheerfully talking to a couple of faithful patrons of the establishment. His phone rang. It was his mom.

"Emeka, something has happened here in Nigeria. I am with your father…" He could barely hear his mother's words clearly as they did not have the best connection, and it took a while for her to actually say the words he never thought he'd hear—"Your father has passed away."

Emeka dropped his phone on the ground. As he stood there before his guests, he could not believe the words he'd just heard, and the look of sheer horror on his face was so evident that his guests grew immediately concerned about him. Whatever he had just heard on the other end of the phone line had to be very bad news.

Apologizing to his guests, Emeka hurriedly picked up his phone and excused himself. He did not want to affect anyone around him with the tragic news, so he made his way to his office and plopped down in his chair. He was in a state of shock—the kind that produces no tears, just mind-paralyzing numbness. In fact, he did not actually cry until he saw his father being buried more than four weeks later.

"I was a fifth-year senior in college," remembers Nate. "I was at my mom and dad's house off campus that day. For some reason, I was in my mother's bedroom, standing in front of her full-length mirror, checking out my clothes. My cell phone rang. After a few moments, through the muffled static over the phone, I could make out her saying, 'Your dad has passed away.' I remember pausing and trying to process her words. She repeated herself, 'Your dad has passed away.' *My dad died? My dad? Impossible. My dad died? Why? How?* Overwhelmed with emotion, all by myself in the house and alone in the room, I began to cry, collapsing to the soft carpet in convulsive sobbing. I never knew that my dad was sick, so it was a shock. Yes, I knew that my mom went back to Nigeria, but I didn't know she'd gone back because he was sick! After all, Dad had just been home for Onyii's wedding, and after the wedding, I'd driven him to New York's JFK airport to catch his plane back to Nigeria. He was not sick at all at the time. He seemed completely fine. Everything was good. Now this."

As Rose gathered resources to transport her children back to Nigeria for their father's funeral, the family remained close and strong. This was the first they'd ever realized the depth and significance of what it meant to be a family in the sense their father had always described—and what it meant to stick together at all costs. The time, for which their father had prepared them for so long, had finally arrived.

"It wasn't really real," Emeka describes. "In between all the grief and worry and questions surrounding my father's passing, we functioned as a family. We still laughed, fought, and had discussions—we were a unit. We were fully aware that we had the responsibility to continue his legacy and that the responsibility to uphold the family covenant would shift to us. When my father made a covenant with God, we made a covenant with God. The work he had begun had to continue in us, and we could only do this by sticking together."

It was not until months later that the family would see Apollos's body at his funeral in Nigeria. Rose was faced with seeing to the care of her deceased husband, returning to the U.S. to prepare her children for travel, making funeral arrangements, and returning to Nigeria for the funeral. This activity required much coordination and organization. Most of all, however, it required much time.

"During this waiting time," David explains, "I simply told my mind that my father was still in Nigeria working at the school. The whole time, all I did was replay what he said to me about keeping the family together. I had to be strong for the family, so that whole time, I didn't shed a single tear—until the funeral."

The trip back to Nigeria to see their father's burial several weeks after his passing was a surreal one for the Ihedigbos. It was a passionate, moving one that they would never forget.

"The trip that we took to Nigeria for my dad's funeral was completely different from the trip we'd taken several years prior," reflects Nate. "That first trip was a blast, but this trip was all business. We didn't even go to the village. My mom was very protective over us, so we stayed at the hotel, took care of the necessary funeral arrangements, and then left. The funeral itself was so emotional. We broke down in tears as we saw my father out in the elevated casket surrounded by a lot of people—a *lot* of people. Our family members from Nigeria kept telling us to stop crying because my dad had gone on to a better place, but it was so difficult not to cry because of what he meant to our lives. However, rather than focus on the people there, we chose to focus on bonding among ourselves as brothers and sister."

"It hit me hard," remembers David. "We were under the burial tent, and I was fine until it was time to walk around and view the body. The closer and closer I got to the body, the more tears I let go. For the very first time since my father's death, I cried and cried and cried. I knew that we were supposed to keep the line moving, but I just couldn't move. I just stood there. I froze. My uncle said, 'David, you have to move.' but all I could do was cry and stare. My mom told him to just let me stand there while all of the other people moved around me. For the first time, I couldn't believe that my father had actually passed away. After we buried my father, keeping my mom strong and being by her side for anything she needed was my priority in life. I didn't move out of the house until I was twenty-six years old. The reason was I didn't want to leave my mom alone until she got strong enough for me to leave her. I was willing to do whatever it took and stay however long I needed to stay."

"The only memory I have in my head from my dad's funeral in Nigeria was the part of the funeral when you walk by to view the body," recalls James. "All I remember is me and my brothers standing at the head of the casket, looking down at him and hugging one another. That was the first time we said, 'Four equals one.' The four of us equals my dad. It meant that we would honor the sacrifice that my dad put into place to keep our family together and that we would always make sure that our family was provided for. That is the same task we have today—to stay a family, always be there for each other, stay close, and talk or communicate every day. This is the reason why there is not a day that goes by when I don't speak to my siblings. Every day we look over each other. Every single day."

As her children went through their own grieving process, Rose had to not only ensure that her children were comforted but deal with her own heartbreak at the loss of her life's companion. She loved the fact that her son David and the rest of her children offered her all the love and sympathy a mother could ask for; however, at the death of her husband, the only real, true consolation she could find was when she looked up to the Lord, believing he would take care of the family. In light of now being the single parent of five children, she expressed optimism in the face of tragedy and moved on with her life.

Apollos Ihedigbo was a one-eyed narcoleptic that came from a single family in the Nigerian village of Umuawa, and though he was deemed least likely to succeed, millions of households around the world pay homage to him at least once a week between the months of August and February as they shout his name: I-hed-*digg*-bo! I-hed-*digg*-bo! I-hed-*digg*-bo! This is quite a legacy.

If you were to ask close acquaintances of Apollos to close their eyes and describe the first three things that come to mind about a legend, their responses tend to fall into the same ballpark: Apollos praising God and leading Bible study, Apollos loving his children, and Apollos giving of his life so that others could live better ones. The only thing he'd ever discussed leaving for his children was the spiritual importance of walking with the Lord—that they would live lives before God that were pleasing to Him. To Apollos, this is the greatest legacy of all.

NATAC TODAY: MORE THAN TWO THOUSAND LIVES CHANGED AND COUNTING

If you ever find yourself riding through the busy streets of Nigeria in the city of Umuahia, on Item Street, a slight turn to your left will reveal NATAC. Though its founder has passed away, his vision still stands. A testament to that vision sits right within the school's door; when guests enter, they see a handsome picture of Dr. Apollos Ihedigbo surrounded by pictures of some of the students whose lives have been changed for the better as a result of the school's programs.

Today, NATAC remains a fully functional technical school in Umuahia. When it opened, it was the only one of its kind in the city; however today, there are several other schools like NATAC in the area providing lots of competition. Nonetheless, NATAC continues to grow each year, experiencing a constant flow of students who have witnessed the impact that the school has made in the lives of their own friends, family members, and acquaintances.

By the end of 2011, more than 2,050 students had graduated from NATAC's programs since its opening in 2009. This number is still growing as the school continues to thrive and educate the Nigerian public. A dedicated staff currently serves the organization, providing administrative and instructional services for students who enroll.

Despite the fact that the school's programs were downsized to some degree after Apollos's passing, much of the same programming that he began at NATAC still continues today. In the current facility, one will find administrative offices, computer technology classrooms, and computer engineering classrooms where students learn how to fix and maintain computers. A very diverse student body traffics in and out of the doors of NATAC. Professionals (in their twenties, thirties, and forties), lawyers, and doctors who enter the program simply to gain the knowledge of how to fix and maintain their own computers, high school dropouts, high school graduates on the way to college, second-career starters—anyone can benefit from NATAC.

Graduation from a school like NATAC offers benefits that are two-fold. First, attending the school's programs positions those in need of remedial education to retake basics like English, math, and science in order to either gain admission into a four-year college or university or to place out of these courses once they are admitted. Then attending the school's computer technology program positions graduates to obtain better jobs, higher promotions, and sometimes, simply increased skill levels for their own personal use. Some students with a more entrepreneurial gene have even graduated from NATAC and went on to create their own jobs, opening up their own computer institutes where other students go to learn about computers, while others go on to excel through promotions at their jobs.

Regardless of the certification track they choose, NATAC students must make a six-month commitment to a program of study, attending classes five days a week from morning until evening in order to earn their certification diploma. Understanding the lives of busy professionals, the school also offers accelerated intensive study programs that include extended evening hours and weekend study, allowing them to complete their program in only three months.

Dr. Rose Ihedigbo is still the most hands-on family member when it comes to NATAC, intent on carrying out the legacy she and her husband began. After Apollos' passing, she'd taken leave of her job for an extended stay in Nigeria. Prior to this, aside from the three-month leave of absence she'd taken when they had first established the school together, the complete workings of NATAC had been under her late husband's doing, and it was now time for her to establish her own presence at the school.

Taking leave from her job in 1995, Dr. Ihedigbo traveled to Nigeria with eighteen-year-old Onyii and seventeen-year-old Emeka in tow, choosing to only bring her two oldest children along for the journey. Emeka remembers being impressed as he watched his mother navigate the Nigerian system to advance her vision of the school.

"My mother took us with her as she made her rounds taking care of all of the technical logistics for NATAC," Emeka recounts. "We went to different agencies, offices, and the ministries of education to complete the paperwork. I was moved at how my mom was able to talk to the various officials and make things happen. It is a unique culture, so sometimes it took a bribe, and other times, it took outright negotiating ability. On one occasion, when she was negotiating to lease a new building for the school, they said that they would allow her to lease the building as long as their kids could go to the school. Whatever it required, my mom took care of business and made things happen."

Patrick, the board director of Friends of NATAC in the U.S. had the privilege of traveling to Nigeria and seeing his friend in action in 2001. "When Dr. Ihedigbo goes to Nigeria to check on the project, she commands respect. If anything is awry, she corrects it and they listen and follow. She is very much the executive director of the school. Dr. Ihedigbo was in the background when we started, but when her time came, she stepped confidently forward. She too believes it is God's work and should be done."

Dr. Ihedigbo's job at the Massachusetts Society for the Prevention of Cruelty to Children (MSPCC) as director of the early intervention program was highly supportive of her repeated leaves to see after the school—two weeks leave here, a month's leave there. Her coworkers and supervisors were aware that more than just a mere service project, this was a family's life's work. Today, Dr. Ihedigbo is a self-employed, independent consultant, a career that allows her the freedom and independence to go to Nigeria and stay as long as necessary to oversee NATAC's various projects.

With each trip to Nigeria, new progress is made towards advancing the school's vision. Of her frequent international journeys to oversee the college, she explains, "Whenever I travel back to the school, they know I am from the U.S. and they expect me to bring things with me. I always ship lots of books, and they make a big difference. I also bring computers and funds to buy things like technology parts and equipment. Recently, we paid for an Internet café to be installed in the school, but it is open to members of the public who will come and pay to use it. We also have a business center in the school with a Xerox machine and printers. People can bring their materials to be typed and printed, and these supplemental enterprises help to pay salaries and sustain the school."

The future of NATAC is bright. Dr. Ihedigbo and the NATAC family are actively involved in raising funds necessary to purchase land for a new school location—a free-standing vocational building away from the hustle and bustle of the city that they will own instead of renting. In addition to computer repair and technology, this new campus will focus on another key aspect of education for Nigerians: agriculture.

While an agricultural focus has always been in the vision of the Nigerian-American Technical and Agricultural College, when Apollos passed, this aspect of the school's programming was put on temporary hold; implementing it would require one of the Ihedigbos being on the ground in Nigeria providing direction, support, and supervision for it. At the time, Rose was attending to her grieving family, providing comfort and care as she watched over each child individually as any good mother would. However, the plans towards establishing an agricultural office for NATAC are in full swing again—the season of grief for their husband and father has ended, and in his honor, the family now focuses on perpetuating his legacy.

The agricultural focus that will be developed as the next phase of NATAC is a critical one for the advancement of Nigeria, as agricultural training is a great need. With the implementation of its new program, the school will focus on the food production, preservation, nutrition, and other aspects that will teach individuals and communities how to engage in sustainable agricultural practices. Through the successful procurement of partners and supporters who recognize the critical need for such programming, NATAC will be able to establish the agricultural training as a two-year associates degree of technology and agriculture that would be transferable to four-year colleges and universities both within Nigeria and even to institutions in the United States. The ability to offer such a degree will also give NATAC a significant advantage over the other competitor colleges offering small-scale computer training to Nigerians. By developing individual minds with this vital training, the Ihedigbos hope to help develop a nation.

To date, there are many success stories that surround NATAC's current level of programming—stories that would make Apollos proud of the legacy for which he'd so diligently labored and sacrificed to bring to pass. For example, there is the story of one student that Dr. Rose met in 2009.

"Dr. Ihedigbo, there is someone here to whom I would like to introduce you," the site supervisor called out as she walked into the warm NATAC building. There was no central air-conditioning, only fans to control the heat in the classrooms so that the students could focus on their lesson. The cement floors did not help the situation much, as the tenacious Nigerian heat radiated upwards from them. She dabbed the sweat from her forehead before her introduction and stepped into his office. It was cooler there.

"Dr. Ihedigbo," he said as he stood to his feet and pointed with a palm-upwards open hand to a smartly dressed gentleman who also rose to his feet, "I would like you to meet Paul, a former NATAC graduate." Dr. Ihedigbo reached out to shake the young man's hand. He had a nice, firm handshake, which was a testament to his training and professionalism.

"Ahhh, a NATAC graduate! Pleased to meet you," she replied.

"Dr. Ihedigbo, I would like to tell you my story," the man began. "I attended NATAC a couple of years ago and completed your six-month program. After I learned valuable knowledge here, I left the city and found a job working as an office administrator—a very nice job with very nice pay that I was only able to get because of what I learned in your school. After I got my nice job, I met a beautiful woman and got married, and then there is this," he said as he began to slowly made his way towards the office door. "May I show you something outside, Dr. Ihedigbo?"

"Sure, sure," she replied, not sure of what awaited her. They stepped outside of the school's door. The young man pointed towards a very nice car that was parked in front of the NATAC building.

"That is my car! Mine! My car!" he exclaimed as he pointed to himself as the proud owner. "I could have been living on the street, trying to survive in poverty, or even trapped in a dead-end job, but I thank God I went to NATAC!" he shouted with both hands raised in the air in a sincere praise to God.

Witnessing this man's live testimony was mind blowing for Dr. Rose. To see a life standing before her, one that had been changed by her family's dream and sacrifice, one that had fared so well as a result of what he'd learned in her school, and most of all, one that had come back to say thank you was overwhelming.

She hugged him tightly and thanked him for returning to share his story.

Then there was the success story of the young woman that Dr. Rose met during her trip to NATAC in March 2010.

Dr. Rose wheeled her bag into the Nigerian hotel in the city of Umuahia, one of the biggest and nicest in this capital city of Abia State. She had arrived at the hotel via the NATAC supervisor who had picked her up from the airport. After almost twenty hours of air travel, she was quite exhausted, and her face told the story of her fatigue. Nonetheless, there was lots of work to do, so she decided that she would brisk through check-in, freshen up a little, and then have the supervisor drive her to NATAC to begin checking things out at the school.

As she approached the check-in counter, the hotel manager saw her and made a beeline in her direction.

"Dr. Ihedigbo!" he exclaimed. "Welcome back to Umuahia! How are you?" he asked.

"Oh, I'm blessed...truly happy to be back," she replied. "God has blessed me with His traveling mercies, and now I am here and ready to hit the ground to get to work at NATAC," she said with an enthusiasm that belied the obvious fatigue in her eyes.

"Praise the Lord," said the manager. "Dr. Ihedigbo, before you check in, I would like to introduce you to someone if I may," he requested.

"Sure, sure," Dr. Ihedigbo acquiesced. Though she was tired, she was always polite. The manager led her in the direction of the front desk and nodded in the direction of the woman who stood before them in a very sharp, business-suit-like hotel uniform.

"Dr. Ihedigbo, please meet one of your former NATAC graduates. After she graduated from your program, she beat out all of the competition to secure this job as the front desk manager of the hotel." With a big smile that seemed to release all of the exhaustion her body held, Dr. Ihedigbo reached out and shook the young lady's hand. The NATAC supervisor who had been standing just behind Dr. Ihedigbo shook the young lady's hand too.

"Well, congratulations, young lady," she said. "It looks like your NATAC education paid off nicely for you." She was impressed by the graduate that stood before her.

"Yes, Dr. Ihedigbo," the young woman started, "NATAC was a very positive experience for me, and it gave me the advantage to be able to earn such a good job. Thank you for your school."

As Dr. Ihedigbo completed her check-in and rolled her large suitcase towards the staircase, she did so with a smile. Usually, her rewards for these long flights and extended stays in Nigeria to work at the college did not come until the very end of her stay. However, this time, her reward came at the beginning with yet another piece of living evidence that her labor was not in vain.

For every NATAC success story that is brought to Dr. Ihedigbo's attention, there are countless others that exist, building better lives for themselves and their families as the result of their matriculation through the Nigerian-American Technological and Agricultural College. Many have used their certificates to secure professional, well-paying jobs, while others have beat out the competition to secure university admission as a result of their extensive knowledge of computers and the educational development they received at NATAC.

In Nigerian thought, real success is not truly success until it is shared with others, and while it would be easy to write off the Ihedigbos' mind-set surrounding success as something uniquely Nigerian, however, it would also be discounting the value of the mind-set. The ability to struggle harder for, endure hardship for, dream for, strive for, and ultimately achieve success is a perspective that is not a uniquely Nigerian one, but a uniquely immigrant one.

In fact, Nate best captures the mind-set in a philosophy he terms the "think like an immigrant" philosophy. To anyone who desires to be successful, especially in America, he would simply encourage them to think like the immigrant.

"When you think like an immigrant," he explains, "you are so gung ho about taking advantage of all of the opportunities available all around you that you don't feel entitled to someone giving you things. You feel like the chances of having them are as good as anyone else's if you put in what it takes to get them: education, hard work, discipline, and determination. Rather than focusing on what you feel entitled to have, take advantage of your desire to achieve. Desire to succeed at all costs, and constantly remind yourself that failure is not an option. Do not allow yourself to have a backup plan. *That* is thinking like an immigrant."

With each Ihedigbo child, there is a fluid consistency in both how to define and how to realize success in life. If you didn't know any better, you would think it was rehearsed over and over again behind the four walls of the family's home in preparation for the day that they had to answer the success question in an interview, but that is not the case. Being reared in a family with two parents who came to the United States having nothing more than a wing and a prayer, two parents who had set their sights on success and were willing to do whatever God told them to do to attain it, including doing what most others are unwilling to do—work harder than those around you, endure lean times with a joyful spirit, and make sacrifices—has rubbed off on their children.

Growing up Nigerian in America came with its own set of built-in cultural expectations and pressures. The standards of achievement to which they are held are no less than those of the typical American family; in fact, they are often greater than the average nonimmigrant family in the U.S.

"We were all raised with similar mind-sets and values," James explains about the company of Nigerians that surrounded him in Massachusetts. "My cousin went to Yale. His sister went to Yale as well, and another one of his sisters went to Amherst College, all Ivy League schools. That was the mind-set we grew up with as second-generation Nigerian-Americans." When James arrived at UMass, he found other Nigerians who held the same standards of accomplishment. "The Nigerians I met in college told me the same thing went for them. They would say, 'My parents say I have to be a doctor or a lawyer.' The standards are set high among Nigerians as a rule, especially since all our parents worked so hard to give us an opportunity to get educated and have a better life— a better one than they had."

While some might consider this constant emphasis on achievement and success to be too much undue pressure for a youngster, the Ihedigbos siblings were quite different. "My parents taught us to have a will not to be average, to have a will to succeed at everything you do. It is empowering that you have to be the best," explains David. "Success has been instilled in us since we were very small. Failure is not an option, and we were not even allowed to entertain the idea of failing because the only option was to succeed. For all of our years, our parents said this to us over and over again, and even today, it comes as second nature to us."

For example, in James's mind, the Nigerian mind-set is about seizing opportunities. "Opportunity is the key to life, no matter what the circumstance. Everyone who is successful was given an opportunity. Nigerians seize the opportunity in front of us. Americans often have opportunity—even greater ones than Nigerians have—but they tend to complain so much about the circumstances and obstacles around them instead of just seizing the opportunity."

James also recognizes that his mind-set about what it takes to get where you desire to be in life is due to his upbringing and that he is a product of an environment that shaped his mentality into one that is willing to do whatever it takes to get there. "If you live in a village in Nigeria, the kind of village that is so far out that you have to walk three miles to get water, and someone offers you a job at a hotel to iron clothes, you'd take it! You run with it and become the best you can be at your job. In America, you can be in the middle or lower class and be given an opportunity to work at Wendy's, but instead of seizing the opportunity, becoming your best, and working your way up, you either pass up the job or you take it but see yourself as being stuck there. You don't do your best. It's all about your mind-set."

Overall, the Ihedigbos remain focused on the true, genuine definition of success.

"My mom always says, 'I'm so happy that I get to brag about my children and their success,' but I'm proud to brag about my parents and their successes. When I actually realized they'd left Nigeria, gotten their education, and went back to establish a school in Nigeria, I was so proud. So many people leave that context in Nigeria and never ever go back. I'm as proud as a person could be to come from such a family," says James.

David sums up the Ihedigbo family's views of success, perhaps the best, when he explains, "The biggest thing about our success story is not about the jobs we have or even about James playing in the NFL. Instead, it is more about the underlying principles that we stand for and what we are trying to do as a family. The fact that my parents have put a college in Nigeria that is made for people to develop educationally so that they can better themselves is the big story. Our family foundation, HOPE Africa, that James is the president of is the big story. We bring hope and scholarship to people so they can have a brighter future. Thus, we do not define ourselves by the money we make or the fame that surrounds us, but by the number of people whose lives we touch on a daily basis."

Today, thousands of people around the world cheerfully shout the Ihedigbo name, not only because they see the youngest in the family making hard tackles on the field but because they see their own lives that were impacted by the family who dared to offer them an education—and a *hope*.

JAMES IHEDIGBO: MAKING AN IMPACT ON AND OFF THE FIELD

Without a doubt, the most notable success story in the Ihedigbo family is that of NFL veteran, James Ihedigbo. After being a stand-out football player and graduating from Amherst Regional High School in 2001, James attended the University of Massachusetts and earned degrees in sociology and criminal justice.

Ever since he was a smaller-than-average member of his local neighborhood's pee wee football team roster, James had wanted to play in the NFL. Dreams and visions of emulating the heroes that he saw on *Monday Night Football* bolt into the end zone with lightning speed filled his sleeping and waking hours. "I remember watching Emmitt Smith running the football for fifty yards, and when he got close to the end zone, he waved. The next game, I ran a sixty-yard touchdown and did the same thing—I waved. I wasn't trying to taunt the other players, I was just emulating Emmitt Smith," he recalls.

Some breaks come easily for some people, and others are forced to put in extra work to be recognized—they simply have to work a little harder. This may seem unfair or like a bad break to some, but to James Ihedigbo, it's par for the course. Not only is he used to having to work harder, it was ingrained into him by his mother and father that he must do whatever it takes to succeed, as long as it does not compromise his faith in Christ. For James, this has included working longer and harder than others in order to attain his desired outcome. Sacrifice is the name of the game, and no wonder—he saw his parents do it, and they reached their desired outcome, and he exercised the principle throughout his lifetime and experienced the same result. Hard work pays off. This makes James Ihedigbo far from your average guy—far from typical.

"I don't think I'm typical at all," James explains. "The story behind my family and NFL career is what makes me so different. My family has always had to work for everything we've gotten in life, and I've had to do the same in football. I had to walk on to the team at UMass, prove myself, and earn a scholarship. I had to try out for the New York Jets, prove myself, and earn a contract. When I came to the NFL, there were guys who had been second-round draft picks who ended up getting cut and ending their career, while I tried out, worked harder and longer and am still playing. My mentality makes me different."

James is not afraid of going the extra mile because it is this extra mile that has taken him far beyond his dreams of being a professional football player, elevated him to a national platform, featured him on national television shows, and included him in spreads in national magazines.

"My mentality is that you have to outwork everyone," he explains. "There are so many people faster than me and better players than me, but I outwork them to have the upper hand. Every day, I make a pledge to be dedicated, motivated, and determined to pursue greatness. I'm not afraid to be great and to pursue opportunities to have a great career, God willing." These are not the words of a typical pro athlete, whose words are characteristically proud and boastful, and James recognizes this; he knows that he is different.

"I'm different because my values are different. My mom always said, 'Blessed are the meek for they shall inherit the earth.' This has taught me that I must remain humble and grateful for the place that I am in and that I'm no more important than any other person. I just have a different career. Football is what I do for a career, not who I am."

When you flip on the local sports network and watch the rotating loop of sports recaps and highlights for the day, you will witness many pro athletes, when asked about the secret of their success, explaining that mysterious "something on the inside" that drives them, that "gutsy determination" that they were inherently born with, that "self-made, self-reliant" attitude that developed when they realized that everything they would become was up to them because they had no one else. However, this mentality doesn't appear in James's playbook. Instead, he references watching his mother and father's motivation and drive to develop themselves in order to create a better life for their family, always fighting, always hoping, always praying, and as a result, always achieving—and he simply followed suit.

When other people call James Ihedigbo successful, their definition of his success simply does not register. Rather, he prefers to define his own success. For James Ihedigbo, success is measured by setting the bar high and achieving his goals so that he can re-adjust the bar to an even higher level. He makes a goal, he achieves the goal, he pats himself on the back, and then he sets another goal—a higher one. Only by gaining mastery over each self-imposed challenge does James feels a level of personal success.

"I learned how to be successful by watching my parents set goals and achieve those goals, no matter how high. My dad came from Nigeria and earned a doctorate at UMass and then went on to found a college in Nigeria. My mom came from Nigeria with little education, earned her way to a doctorate degree at UMass, and has been at the top of her career in education for thirty years. They set these goals and not only met them but surpassed them. They reached the highest point you can reach in education." As a result of his parents' example, James strives to be the best and reach for the highest level of accomplishment in his own pursuits.

"I now judge myself through their drive and set my goals by the same standards they did. Being an NFL player is great, but can you be the best? Being a philanthropist through my foundation is great, but can you be one of the best organizations out there that touches lives around the world? Success for me is not accomplishing ordinary goals, but being the best in anything that I do. Success is the pursuit of greatness."

Music lovers or not, each of us has a soundtrack that we listen to every day of our lives. This soundtrack loops over and over in our heads, day in and day out, and provides the background music that influences the thoughts we think, the places we go, and the decisions we make. When we are born, the tracks are empty; as we grow, through constant repetition and reinforcement, our environments lay down tracks that shape our mentalities and guide our thoughts and actions as we walk through life. The key track on James Ihedigbo's soundtrack is this: to whom much is given, much is expected. The voice behind the track: Apollos Ihedigbo. Prior to his passing, Apollos engrained this over and over again into his son, and as a result, this track plays out in James's subconscious every waking moment of his life.

Scan the players' guests section at any game that has James's number on the home or away team roster, and you will find Rose, jumping up and down and rallying the crowd at the top of her small but high-pitched voice. This proud NFL mom is sure to be clad from head to toe in her son's team colors with the Ihedigbo name proudly displayed on her back. She wants the world to know of the son that God blessed her with—a son that does not hesitate to give Him glory through his life on the playing field.

James is keenly aware of his mother's presence, and even though he cannot make out her voice among the tens of thousands of other die-hard football fans screaming in the stadium, he knows she is there, keeping her section pumped up whether his team is winning or losing.

"My mom is my biggest fan," he says. "She hasn't miss a game *ever*. Every game. Even when I played Pop Warner little league, she'd hop in the car and drive us every game. When I played for UMass in college, she made it to every game, whether at Boston, Villanova, or even the national championship in Tennessee. When I began playing for the New York Jets in the NFL, she was there, traveling as far as Miami or San Diego. If there's a game, she's there. Regardless of where I'm playing, my mom is going to be on a flight or in a car flying or driving to wherever the game is."

Mom is not alone in the stands at James's games; his brothers commonly attend the games along with Mom, so wherever the NFL game of the week takes them, they make the gridiron event a family affair. The Ihedigbo brothers round out the pack in the stands, shouting along with millions of other fans as their baby brother makes impressive hard tackles and defends his quarterback. They're all present and accounted for, proudly sporting the name Ihedigbo in the team's colors. This makes James feel special, as it would any man; no matter how big, strong, and tough a man is, everyone wants to be supported and supported, cheered on, and encouraged by those whom he loves most. For James, this is his family.

Brother Emeka left Massachusetts in 2011 to be closer to his brother and be able to attend all of his games, writing in his employment contracts wherever he goes the stipulation that he must be able to leave during game time to go be with his brother. Regardless of where he is, he makes it his duty to hop a train, a bus, or hop in the passenger seat of someone's car the night before or the morning of a game so that he can be present in the stands as his brother takes the field. More than a duty, however, it is a privilege for him to be there—as much as it is a privilege for James.

"It makes me feel kind of privileged. It's an awesome feeling when you wear the Ihedigbo last name on the back of your jersey and your family members are wearing the same thing, cheering for you and proud of you. It makes you want to represent," say James. "After the game, David will come to me and say, 'You don't know how many people asked me where they could get an Ihedigbo jersey.' It makes him feel really proud of me, and it makes me feel really proud that he's proud of me."

The fun for the Ihedigbo clan does not end after the game is over; in fact, it's just beginning. Freshly showered out of the locker room, instead of heading for the nightclub to celebrate as is the custom for many other professional athletes, James makes a beeline for whatever restaurant his clan has agreed upon for dinner to enjoy some good food and spending time with his family. Win or lose, they gather around the table and enjoy the close-knit company of one another.

Any observer standing outside of the restaurant window watching the group around the table would witness what is obviously a family (as they all bear the similar strong Nigerian facial features of their parents) enjoying themselves as a boisterous group, laughing loudly and perhaps even a little too rowdy for neighboring tables as they crack jokes, rib one another, and discuss the fun of the day's events in their full-volume, powerful Nigerian accents.

The siblings would agree that the most rowdy representative of the postgame table is Nate. Though he offers the least in stature as the smallest family member at the table, he is the most provocative. With the sharpness of the Nigerian mind, he accesses everything that his brain has recorded over the course of the day in an instant, waits for just the right moment, and then uses the succulent, juicy bit of information to push someone's button at the table—all for the family's entertainment. Satisfied with the new fireworks his latest button push is about to launch, he then sits back and watches them fly around the table. He's actually quite genius at it, though his brothers would prefer that he use his powers for good rather than this kind of humorous entertainment. After the fireworks sizzle out, Nate strategizes who will be the butt of the humor behind his next button push. Push, jab, and repeat—all for the family's postgame fun and entertainment as they celebrate the on-field accomplishments of their brother James.

At some point, in the midst of the celebration, the brothers look for the moment where they will offer some level of critique of James's play for the day. They all try to take some credit in getting him where he is today. Helping to provide direction, coaching, and support for years, each Ihedigbo male feels like he has had a strong hand in the success of James's football career; providing this same level of guidance during his NFL career seems natural. Valuing the insights of his brothers, James listens intently as they begin to engage in an analytical discussion of what he did right, what he did wrong, and what he should correct for the next game.

"In the first quarter, the block that you threw, you laid that guy out. That was unbelievable! On the flip side, though, you should have gotten the quarterback. Watch that film and you'll get it right next time."

Their analysis is not wasted on their baby brother; Emeka, Nate, and David's words have an abiding impact on his thought process and the way he plays on the field. With maturity, he listens and nods as his brothers try to make him a better player, analyzing every move play by play. Being such a diligent worker, the next time, you can bet he will get things right. After the family dinner, the family always prays.

The family ends the drawn-out dinner with a toast. Saying their good-byes to one another in a sea of hugs for the brothers and kisses for their mother, they go their separate ways—that is, until the next game when they will reunite.

Every football player that sets foot on the playing field dreams of one day going professional in his athletic career, playing for one of his favorite NFL teams, and going to the big dance—the Super Bowl. For James, on Sunday, February 5, 2012, one of his lifelong dreams came true. As he walked onto the field at Lucas Oil Stadium in Indianapolis, Indiana suited up to play in Super Bowl XLVI, the years of hard work, discipline, dedication, and persistence had finally paid off. Considering that only 2 percent of college football players actually make it to the NFL and that, with average team rosters of fifty players for each of the thirty-two NFL teams, James recognized that he was blessed to be one of the more than 1,600 players—less than 1 percent of men that play in the NFL—to take the Super Bowl field. He realized that he had been highly favored, and he remembered what he'd known all along—he was blessed.

This favor that culminated in his arrival at Super Bowl XLVI had been building for some time. On March 11, 2011, due to a labor dispute between NFL league owners and players, a lock-out began. After eighteen weeks and four days of bargaining and negotiating, the lockout eventually came to an end. During the time of this sensitive clash between players and the establishment, free agents like James were in limbo; however, unlike other free agent players who endured the more than four months of intense disagreements with nail-biting worry and excruciating uncertainty about the future, James was at peace. He knew that God had something waiting for him around the corner, and whatever it was, it was His best.

After the lockout ended, surprisingly, James was not re-signed with the Jets; now for several weeks with no offer on the table to play for the upcoming season, he had to patiently wait on God—and always on time, God showed up.

In August 2011, less than one month before the season opener, free agent James Ihedigbo was signed to the New England Patriots. In being selected to play for his hometown team, he was prouder than ever before to don the red, white, and blue Patriots uniform that he so admired as they used to dance across the screen while he, his brothers and sister, and his mother and father sat on the edge of the family sofa glued to the television. Now he had come full circle, and he, the hometown hero of Amherst, was playing in his own backyard. What a moment.

The moment escalated to new levels as the Patriots fought for a winning season, won the playoffs, and landed a spot in the game of all games—the Super Bowl. After only one season with his hometown team, James was living out the dreams of every well-padded, cleat-wearing player who dared to dream such a career highlight as this. Some say that it was his hard work, his dedication to training and his discipline that landed him on this particular team, in this particular place, at this particular time, and they would be right—but only in part. If you ask James, these things were foundational, but it was his faith that led him here to the big dance, and it is his faith that will continue to lead him on and off the field.

Unfortunately, the New England Patriots experienced a disappointing defeat at the hands of the New York Giants with a score of 21–17. However, it was a valiant fight—one that James looks forward to one day fighting again for an encore presentation at the Super Bowl. However, James was waived by the Patriots on August 31, 2012 and picked up a few days later by the Baltimore Ravens. "it has gone well, " he said of joining the Ravens. " I worked my butt off to learn the defense and execute it. I am playing with a great bunch of guys here with a relentless attitude. It is an honor to be a part of it."

On February 3, 2013, Ihedigbo and the Baltimore Ravens would make his second Super Bowl appearance, Super Bowl XLVII.

🍂

James is not lax in fulfilling his commitment to use his platform as an NFL player to give back to others. In support of the vision of NATAC and other educational opportunities for advancing the educational prospects of Nigerian students, in 2008, James and his mother, Rose, cofounded HOPE Africa, a nonprofit charitable organization that is designed to *help our people excel* by providing opportunities for advancement to fellow Africans.

With the mission of helping our people excel, HOPE Africa is a public charity driven by three major outcome-based components: scholarship, community engagement, and sustainability. Funded by corporate and private donations, the organization strives to provide full-ride scholarships to both NATAC and universities in the United States. While NATAC remains in Nigeria, HOPE Africa is worldwide.

In an effort to teach each student the essential need of adopting the Ihedigbos' creed of "You're not successful until you have given back to your community," students are required to couple their education with volunteerism—this addresses HOPE Africa's community-engagement component. As such, HOPE scholarship recipients that live in the U.S. couple their education with volunteerism in whatever field of study that matches their educational pursuit; if they are studying medicine, for example, they would volunteer in a hospital or other medical facility.

Finally, HOPE Africa's sustainability component is served by the fact that every youth that benefits from the organization must return back to Africa to share the fruits of their education and engagement in the community with those in their homeland—

just like Apollos and Rose did. By this, the legacy of the Ihedigbo endures and is perpetuated by others around the world.

Of all of the accomplishments of her children, it is their involvement in giving back to the people of Nigeria of which she is most proud. "Their success is complete!" she explains. "Each and every one of the children has embraced the vision of going back to Nigeria and fulfilling that educational goal and vision that we have. We are as a whole family unit supporting HOPE Africa," she shares proudly.

James serves as the president, and Rose serves as the cofounder of HOPE Africa and the president of NATAC.

"We are all part of the dream to give back to NATAC through HOPE Africa. Whether we are supporting students in Africa or in the U.S., we are working together, and that is what is most important," explains Dr. Ihedigbo.

In order to engage students around the world with the opportunity to further their education in the United States, HOPE Africa's model is to connect with high school students who are interested in studying abroad in the States and to also partner with well-established, reputable organizations that are already working with young people in the country of origin.

Like many well-meaning organizations beginning their work in Africa, when HOPE Africa first began, its model was to identify students who were interested in furthering their education, screen their grades, educational and community accomplishments, and character, and then once approved, award them scholarships to further their education. HOPE Africa's model is one of guided progression.

When an African student desires to gain entry into the U.S. to study, obtaining the proper approvals to build the bridge from their tiny village to a bustling university in the States is no small, simple prospect. Consequently, another element of HOPE Africa's operations is to work directly with top-ranked colleges and universities to help African students gain admission at negotiated, lower tuition rates while working hand in hand with the students to obtain an educational visa that will make traveling to study at the selected college or university possible. As it is necessary for each international student that travels to study in the U.S. to have a sponsor, HOPE Africa serves as that sponsor, providing the assurance to authorities that it will pay for educational and living expenses until the student's point of graduation. It is the organization's goal to sponsor at least five to six students each year for a four- to five-year education through tax-deductible donations made to the organization and through registration proceeds generated from James's annual NFL summer football camps in the U.S.

For students studying in the States from Nigeria, opportunities abound in their homeland to give back to the African nation they love. The current president of Nigeria, aptly nicknamed Good Luck Jonathan, for all of the good fortune he has enjoyed in being able to progress the country, makes efforts to place a strong focus on energy, water, waste management, and education. As a result, American-educated African students have a prime opportunity to translate their learning into prime positions in both the government and the private sector. HOPE Africa works directly with the leaders and key players within these industries to make the return of their students and their entry into prime jobs available in their sectors a smooth, seamless one. Returning to Africa after the successful completion of a U.S. education is always the plan for these students, and the returns are always made worth their while.

This is in fact the predominant way in which Nigerians tend to define *success*. When a student leaves their country to study in the United States, that student is not considered successful because of what they wear or how they live. Nigerians want to know if they were trained in school with a good education—that is success. They also want to know if they trained their children to understand that even though they were born in America, they are from Nigeria—that is success. Finally, and most importantly, they want to know that those who have left Nigeria will return, their children included, to help their country. To Nigerians, closing the loop is the true measure of success.

Investing in an aspiring student's education in order to equip him or her to give back to the world is the aim of the Ihedigbos' HOPE Africa. This is the same model that was used to bring their father from Nigeria to New York's Houghton College to study, and it is one that they desire to share with the rest of the world. Just as the investment of others helped to change the lives of Apollos and Rose, the Ihedigbos are changing the lives of others, one international education at a time.

In March 2011, James accompanied his mother and a hand-picked delegation of other NFL players, including Amobi Okoye, Connor Bowen, and others, and traveled to Lagos, Nigeria, for almost two weeks. During this trip, which was also supported by the Amobi Okoye Foundation (a close partner of HOPE Africa for years), HOPE Africa conducted a health clinic and American football camps for local children. These camps were not simply for teaching athletic drills on how to move faster and score a touchdown; they were laced with important lessons such as the importance of education, teamwork, and the tenacity to pursue goals.

The five large men drew stares and looks of wonderment as they walked through the five-star hotel lobby in Abuja, Nigeria's capital, and out the front door to the waiting van. They were obviously athletes and obviously not from Nigeria. Whenever such rare specimens came to visit their country, the curious onlookers thought they have come to do good, to give back in some kind of humanitarian way. As the van navigated the loud, bustling Nigerian traffic, the privileged NFL players could not help but feel an overwhelming sense of gratitude for the lives they led back home in the U.S. The closer they arrived to the village areas and the poverty that marked these settlements, the more they realized how blessed they truly were.

The sight that waited to greet them at the football camp was one they would never forget. There were children so poor that many of them were barefoot and had arrived at the camp with stomachs empty and grumbling, sounding off loudly in protest of a lack of food, and yet the smiles on the faces of these kids were the largest, widest, and most genuine these men would ever behold. They were excited beyond words to participate in such an event, meeting American football players and learning how to be athletes from them, and while they did not know the names of these friendly giants, they knew of the NFL because its games were televised in Nigeria from time to time. What they did know about the players is that they wore big pads, threw a ball and hit one another for a living. They knew that it was a violent sport, but it was fun—and that was enough.

"Thank you, Uncle! Thank you, Uncle! Thank you, Uncle!" The kids jumped and bounced and grabbed as they expressed their heartfelt thanks for these men taking the time to visit and teach them. The special t-shirts and food that they received from the camp made this day almost like Christmas, and they were overwhelmed with gratitude. As they walked the distance back to their poor makeshift homes, both their bellies and their hearts were filled. It had been an event they would remember for the rest of their lives.

The day they got to work out with real, live American football players was a life-changing day for these young Nigerians, but it was equally life-changing for the celebrity players—in fact, for all in attendance. On the ride back to the hotel, the players expressed how touched they were by the experience. "When you see kids with no shoes running drills with such enthusiasm and excitement, you can't help but be changed. You step back and say, 'This kid has nothing, but he is enjoying every last bit of life. How dare I ever complain about something I don't have in life or about an inconvenience that I have to experience in a life like mine?'" James shares, voicing the shared sentiment of his fellow players.

Despite the fact that this was a nation in which there are no sports complexes for practice, no football teams, and no leagues, in addition to being touched by the children's gratefulness and enthusiasm, the group also left incredibly impressed with the raw athletic talent of the camp's participants. "I was floored by the flat-out athleticism of these guys. If these kids were in the U.S., you would instantly have an all-star team. Their work ethic, natural talent, and desire to learn were second to none." His celebrity friends agreed, as after taking only a couple of days teaching the boys the fundamentals of the game, they stood back to watch them skillfully execute the flag football plays—throwing the ball, running down the sidelines, making touchdowns and even spiking the ball.

"It was amazing to see what a kid could do with a little opportunity," says James. As they worked with the children, James and Amobi were appreciative that both the NFL and another American football league (which plans to begin recruiting for a new American football league in Africa in the near future) had stepped up to provide the funding to bring this camp from idea to reality.

The delegation also visited poor local village schools, bringing with them books to enhance the children's learning. James recalls, "It was amazing to stand there and see these little kids in grade school. I thought about how my dad, my mom, and my brother and sister once sat in those little chairs, and they all had dreams and aspirations to do something great with their lives. It was great to play a part in these children's lives by encouraging them to keep dreaming and believing that they were made to do great things, even though they all came from the poorest of conditions. I said to them, 'Just because you are in the village doesn't mean that you have to stay in the village.' It was very rewarding to touch those lives."

While the NFL delegation engaged children in football drills and distributed books, there was yet another group of mostly African doctors that accompanied them from the U.S. to Nigeria to host medical clinics that offered vaccinations, breast-cancer screenings, various medical tests, and medications for common ailments. Health care in Nigeria is compromised, for lack of a better term, as the local doctor is often not adequately trained, scarce hospitals are merely teaching facilities filled with student-physicians that teach as they go, and patients must bring along their own sanitation tools. Often in these Nigerian hospitals, electrical power is limited or even nonexistent throughout the day. Thus, medical clinics of the sort hosted by HOPE Africa and the Amobi Okoye Foundation are a welcomed sight.

Nigeria's progress was evident upon James's return in 2011. The last time he'd visited had been with the family to bury his father ten years prior, and based upon the conditions he'd experienced at this time, he had carefully warned his NFL delegation about what to expect in his native land. However, James returned to find evidence all around him that spoke to the level of advancement his homeland had undergone. "It was amazing to see the economic change from when I was last in Nigeria because now there were paved roads, streetlights, and five-star hotels. You prepare yourself for a certain way things will be, and it ends up being completely different," he recalls.

James is on a mission to use his success to give back to Nigeria by providing opportunities for other Nigerians to realize their educational and professional dreams. What he has been blessed with, he desires to use to bless many others—to be used by God as a change factor in other people's lives. Using his NFL platform to make an impact in the world is his purpose, and he embraces it with vigor.

CARRYING ON THE LEGACY: THE IHEDIGBO OFFENSIVE LINE

In the end, the Ihedigbo offensive line that remains today to play out the dreams of Ihedigbo legacy is a varied one, each taking an individual path in pursuit of happiness; however, each path eventually merges with the others, and together as one unit, they take a mutual journey towards success. As one team, they work together, they pray together, they celebrate together, and they stick together. Whatever the difficulty facing them, they keep moving in the Lord Jesus Christ.

At the helm as team coach and quarterback is Dr. Rose Ihedigbo herself. There is perhaps no mother on the face of the planet that is more beloved by her children than Rose. Ask her children what they think of her, and you will elicit description after description of the highest accolades to characterize what could only be the best mom to ever bear a child—in her case, four boys and one girl.

As public representative of the team, James expresses all the players' sentiments concerning their quarterback and coach: "Mom is everything. She does it all without even a glimpse of wanting anything in return. All she does, she does out of love, care, concern for us making the right decisions, and wanting us to be knowledgeable. She is the rock of the family."

Player: *Onyinyechi* (God's gift) Deborah Ihedigbo-Brown
Degree/School: BA, Business Administration, University of Massachusetts

City of Residence: Houston, Texas
Codename: The Role Supermodel

Player Bio:

The oldest Ihedigbo child and only girl, Onyinyechi's name means "a gift from God" in Igbo. She boarded the plane with her mother as a three year-old in 1980. The only female in the house besides her mother, she attended the University of Massachusetts and eventually married Humphrey D. Brown III, a strong believer in Christ who is also passionate about ministry and the things of God. Together, in Houston, Texas, they live a comfortable life, laying their own foundation of faith with their three small children, eight-year-old Ejike, five-year-old Chizara, and Chinua, who is less than a year old.

Coach's Analysis:

I thank the Lord that He gave Onyii to me. She looks so much like me in terms of being a kind and devoted wife to her husband, a good mother to her children, and being very hardworking and industrious. Even as a child, Onyii was strong-minded and determined, and she has never been intimidated by anything at all. Sometimes, even today, she is hard headed because she is a perfectionist and wants everything to be just right; despite this, she does a wonderful job caring for her brothers. Being the eldest child means she bears a lot of responsibility to help the family and to model good behavior for her siblings that will guide them in the right direction. When she was a child, she did a good job at this, and she continues to do so today. With all that she has accomplished though, the fact that she has embraced Christ and is living a life of faith in Him is the thing that I'm most proud of. That is true success.

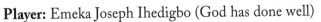

Player: Emeka Joseph Ihedigbo (God has done well)
City of Residence: Jersey City, New Jersey
Codename: The Bear Hugger

Player Bio:

Emeka Joseph Ihedigbo also made the flight to America from Nigeria when he was only a two-year-old toddler. With his passion for culinary arts, he enjoys a successful career in the restaurant service industry as the general manager of a restaurant. Living in New Jersey with his six-year-old son, Simeon, Emeka has also embraced the faith of his parents and uses it to propel him forward in life to touch the lives of other people.

Coach's Analysis:

> I thank God for the success of my son Emeka. He is such a hardworking, intelligent man who has embraced the faith of his parents and loves the Lord. When I think of Emeka as a child, I remember that he was a child that loved to receive attention. He was the one that always cried the most in the house, and I would always wonder why he would cry so much. I finally realized that he really wanted to be touched and loved and that he craved lots of hugs, touches, and attention. He is my loving, affectionate child, and he is still like that today. He is the one that will walk up and give a great big bear hug to anyone he loves. He loves people—all people—and he is the one that will always say, 'Mom, I love you!' All of my kids say 'I love you,' but my Emeka does it differently. He is a special child!

Player: Nathaniel *Chimdi* (my God is alive) Ihedigbo
School: BS in Engineering, University of Massachusetts
MEd, American Intercontinental University, Chicago, IL
City of Residence: Houston, Texas
Code Name: The Peacemaker

Player Bio:

Nathaniel Chimdi Ihedigbo was born in Nigeria and transported to the United States on his mother's lap when he was less than a year old. The apple doesn't fall far from the tree, and in Nathaniel's case, this is not only true genetically, but professionally. His career to become a middle school science teacher was directly influenced by his parents who possessed a love for the field of education. After graduating from the University of Massachusetts with a bachelor's in engineering and from the American Intercontinental University of Chicago with a master's in education, he and his wife, Kara, eventually moved to Houston, Texas, where they now live with their two-year-old Isaiah. They have a particular fondness for children, serving as a coach in the community and mentoring children, especially Nigerians, at any opportunity. He and his household are living happily in Christ, an accomplishment that his mother considers to be his greatest success.

Coach's Analysis:

The highlight of my son's success in life is that he is a believer in Jesus Christ, and I thank God for that. Nathaniel was always a quiet child, and though he did not talk very much, he was always inquisitive, asking lots of questions about famous places and things. When he was young, I also noticed that he had a great curiosity with toys like robots, trains, and remote-controlled cars. It did not surprise me that he pursued engineering in school. He shares my love for education, so he is like me in this regard. However, when I look at him, he is the one that is so much like his father, especially when it comes to peace-making. Nate does not like commotion or fights at all. No matter what you ask him for, he will do it just to maintain the peace. He is my strong, peace-loving child, just like his father, and I have always loved that about him.

Player: David *Ikechukwu* (God's power) Ihedigbo
School: BA, Sports Management, American International College
City of Residence: Jersey City, New Jersey
Team Position: The Glue

Player Bio:

The first Ihedigbo born on American soil, David Ikechukwu Ihedigbo was born in 1981 in North Hampton, Massachusetts. Following the lead of his older siblings, he pursued a college education, graduating from American International College with a bachelor's degree in sports management, training that he used to propel himself into a successful career as a general manager at LA Fitness in Jersey City, New Jersey. Of course, according to Dr. Ihedigbo, this career success pales in comparison to the beauty of his relationship with Jesus Christ, the one thing that makes him a true success.

In the Ihedigbo family, David is the glue—the brother that knows how to talk to each member of the family to calm them down after an argument with another sibling and keep them close. At any given moment, Mom will call him with a request: "I need you to talk to everybody because I don't want people fighting and arguing." Proud to fulfill his father's request of keeping the family together in peace, David will pick up the phone, call each and every person, listen for as long as it takes, and share his father's wisdom with them until everyone is at peace once again.

Coach's Analysis:

> I love the beauty of Jesus Christ in David's humble life, which he lives in devotion to his family and in his aspirations to do more for others. He was always a very compassionate child. Even now, he is still very kind-hearted, hospitable, and loving. He loved his father very much, always being the one to volunteer to be his partner when Apollos wanted to go play tennis. I know that he loves me equally as dearly as he loved his father. When his father passed and I was struggling with his loss, it was David that stayed close to me and watched over me with so much concern and compassion. In fact, he was the last of the children to leave home because he always wanted to stay with me to make sure that I was okay. I love the level of compassion that my son carries for others.

Player: James *Ugochukwu* (the crown of God) Ihedigbo
School: BA, Sociology, University of Massachusetts
City of Residence: Houston, Texas
Team Position: Superstar Baby Brother

Player Bio:

Though he is the youngest of the Ihedigbo clan, James Ugochukwu Ihedigbo has made the Ihedigbo name a famous one in many households across the United States. James excelled in both athletics and school, completing his bachelor's degree in sociology from the University of Massachusetts. In Dr. Ihedigbo's eyes, these are great accomplishments; however, the thing that makes her smile the most about her son is the beauty she sees of Jesus Christ in his life. James wears his relationship with the Lord openly, shining his light as brightly to people who tune in to watch him play across the world as he does to the people that surround him on a daily basis.

Coach's Analysis:

James is the baby, and everybody in the family has always spoiled him. From the time he was born as a young child, we all wanted to baby him and support him, and it is still like that today. We support him in everything he does, and we try to protect him from anything that will hurt him or be too hard on him. As a result, he is the one who always asks for favors and to be supported, and we all comply. After all, he is our baby, so it's hard to say no. Over the years, this has instilled in him a certain level of arrogance, not in a bad way, but in the way that he always expects to have his requests fulfilled. He knows that he is loved and that we'll do anything for him. In fact, he will call and say, 'Hi, Mom, this is your best child calling!' I do not show him any more love than I show my other children, but we do all go out of our way and beyond our means to support him. We still spoil him!

Inside of each team member's home today sits a small wooden statue in the shape of Nigeria—a housewarming gift that Dr. Ihedigbo brought back from Nigeria for her children on one of her many journeys. Inscribed upon each of the small statues are the words, "Nigeria, the Giant of Africa". The first image that comes to mind when the Ihedigbos picture this giant, this great nation, is strength: strength of courage, strength of confidence, strength of spirit, strength of mind, strength of intellect, strength of determination, and strength of survival.

Perhaps most important of all, they cannot help but consider the tremendous strength that lay in the untapped resources and potential of this giant nation. Working together as an offensive team, they have made it their single-focused destiny to do their part to unlock this potential. With Dr. Rose Ihedigbo as their quarterback and the siblings ready to leave it all on the field, there is no way that they will not come out as champions in their endeavor.

The Nigerian-American Technological and Agricultural College is formally registered with the country of Nigeria as Friends of Nigerian People, Inc.; in fact, there is a sign hung outside of the school with this very name that is acknowledged by passersby on a daily basis. As they cross the path of NATAC's front door and glance at this sign, they are reminded each time that this institution was founded by their friends. Real friends. True friends. Friends that never forget you, no matter how successful they become. Friends that do not consider themselves successful until they reach back to help their fellow man with the same opportunities for success.

These friends were Dr. Apollos and Dr. Rose Ihedigbo. For now and forever in the nations' history, they will be known as friends to the people of Nigeria.

WORDS TO LIVE
BY FROM THE IHEDIGBO TEAM

Faith in God

Above all, have faith in God. Without our faith in God, none of us in this family would have achieved anything that we have, because the enemy has always tried to discourage us—but we never gave up. When one door would close, God's grace would open another one. It was our faith that moved us to work hard to achieve our dreams, and God has helped us turn this hard work into the success we all dreamed of.

—James

We have always believed that we can do all things through Christ that strengthens us. Our family being led by Christ has been the critical foundation for our family's success. No matter what, this belief is the anchor that has kept our family together; through Christ, we have learned how to love through anything and how to constantly forgive one another.

—Nate

On What it Takes to Succeed

There are many moving parts to our family's success, but the three biggest factors are clear and simple: unwavering faith in God, hard work, and determination.

—James

Enduring Hardship

Adversity is here to shape us. Always know that all things are working together for our good. Not only for our good but also for the good of others because our lives are a living testimony of how faithful God is. There is always a message in the madness. God is always trying to get you somewhere. He never wants you to stay the same or remain in the same place in life. If we are willing to endure, hardship pushes us closer to our destiny! For whom He for knew He also predestined (Rom. 8:29).

—Onyii

Deep, lasting success will never come quickly or easily; each of us in this family has learned first-hand that it involves a struggle. However, regardless of what obstacles and hardships you have to struggle with, stay focused on the path. Your path may not be the same as someone else's, but your mind-set should be, do whatever work it takes to make it happen, and don't give up on your dream.

—James

Adapt to Your Situation and Make the Best of It

Adapt! When we were thrust into a new culture, we did not shy away from the challenge or give up, we adapted to it. This is something that all immigrant families have to do when they come into a completely new environment. Learning to adapt in transition is going to be key to your ability to see success!

—James

Because we take advantage of every opportunity available to us, our family is like a rose growing out of concrete. My father could have stayed in Nigeria and not fought for a greater future, but he had a vision and decided to pursue that vision with everything he had. That vision brought him to the U.S., and he passed that vision on to us—he blessed all of us with the ability to possess and go after a vision. My father was not a 'now' person, he was a person of the future; he planned for the future, he saved for the future, he invested in the future.

—Nate

Focus on the Goal, Not the Circumstance.

The Lord will provide.

The last time I saw my father was at my wedding 11 years ago. His last advise he gave me was "do not worry, the Lord will provide." I live by that. When stepping out to do something extra ordinary, the natural thing to do is to become anxious and worry about what will happen. Will there be enough? What if this and what if that. What I have learned over the years is truth! The Lord will provide. God wants us to walk in his infinite provision. It is never ending. He will always provide the resources needed for us to complete the tasks that he has called us to.

—Onyii

Always Plan to Give Back

We were always trained that no matter how much, we had to give back, and my father led us in this. He didn't just wake up one day and say, "We're at a point of success now, so we should go back to Africa and give back to our people." No, it was planned from the beginning—from day one—that we would get established and then go back to Nigeria and give back. To whom much is given, much is required, he would say.

—Nate

To whom much is given, much is required. Prepare for success like you expect it every day. Maximize every opportunity you are given. Do what God called you to do. When you are finished and have achieved success, know that it is your responsibility to give back to others who are not as fortunate as you.

—Emeka

Don't Be Afraid to Be Proud of Who You Are

I love being Nigerian. Someone could fill a room up with a hundred different people, and I could easily tell who is Nigerian and who is not. I would instantly be drawn to them, passing by to shake hands with them and call them brother—I would never just walk by. In fact, I would even try to break bread with them. I tell the African kids at the school I teach how to be proud of being African instead of trying to blend in. When I see them, we greet each other and embrace. The African-American kids at the school don't understand this; they wonder how we can take pride in being both Nigerian and American. We embrace our heritage, our ability to trace our ancestry back to the village we came from, and we take pride in who we are. We don't apologize for it, and we certainly do not play it down or hide it!

—Nate

On Being Ordinary and Doing Extraordinary

You don't have to *be* an extraordinary person to *do* extraordinary things. We are just typical people, average Americans. Everything that anyone in my family has accomplished, we accomplished through our faith in God; God did it all. If you can tap into faith in God, He will take you places you had no idea you could go and help you accomplish things you never dreamed you could accomplish.

—David

Always Maintain an Attitude of Gratitude.

I constantly reflect on how my father was the only one out of all of his siblings that was presented the opportunity to come to the states. Naturally, he was poor. He came from a small village. He fetched water each morning like all the others in the village. What made him so special? Our family could have easily been there in Nigeria with no true future. But God favored him through faith. It is because of this that I give thanks everyday. God chose to extend the gift of possibility through this family for others.
Seek first the Kingdom and His righteousness and all other things will be added unto you.
I have never seen the righteous forsaken nor his seed begging bread
The Lord will provide.
The world is watching you. Don't act like a fool. Your life is a living testimony of who you are and who's you are.
Always Forgive.
You can't do it alone. Every joint supplies.

—Onyii

On Hard Work

If two very poor Nigerians could travel that many miles to come to the United States, work their way through the educational system, earn doctorates at UMass, and return to their home country to establish a college, all while raising five children on a very tight income, then go on to have successful lives that are driven by a relationship with God and a desire to give back to others, what's stopping you from getting good grades in class, reaching the top in your education, and going as far as you can go in life? Compared to my parents' struggles, the little challenges we face on a daily basis seem so minute. You can get anywhere with hard work and determination. My family is living proof of that.

—David

On Naysayers

We Ihedigbos never worry about ill will. All we can do is what God called us to do, and as long as we are following His direction, He will take care of the rest.

—Emeka

EPILOGUE

Dr. Rose Ihedigbo, now Rose Ihedigbo- Franklin, got remarried to Rev. Riley Franklin in October of 2008. Both live in Abingdon, Maryland.

The Vacation

We finally made it to an unforgettable vacation on June 3 to 8, 2012, in Montego Bay, Jamaica. We were sixteen in number, including Onyii, her husband Humphrey and three children; Emeka and his son; Nathaniel, his wife Kara and child; David and his fiancée; James and his girlfriend, and also husband Riley and myself. James proposed to his girlfriend and became engaged to Brittany during the vacation.

What a great time of happiness, fun and bonding! We are thankful and will always remain grateful to God for what He has done in our lives.

APPENDIX

IGBO CONVERSATIONAL DICTIONARY

EXCHANGING PLEASANTRIES AND ASKING DIRECTIONS

Hello   *Kedú* (keh-DO)

Good morning   *Ibọla chi* (e-BORLA-CHI)

Good evening   *Ézígbó mgbede* (AY-ZEE-GBO MM-GBAYDAY)

Good night   *Ka chi bọ* (KA-CHI-BAW)

Please   *Biko* (BEE-COE)

Thank you   *Daalu/Imela* (DA-LOO/ EE-MEH-LAH)

You're welcome   *Ndéwo* (IN-day-WOAH)

Yes   *Éeyi, Ëhh* (ey, AEH)

No   *Mbà* (IM-BAH)

I'm sorry.   *Ndo, Gbághàrám* (in-DOH, BA-gah-RAM)

My name is...   "*Áhàm bụ* (or *Afam bu*)..." (AH-H a.m. BOO)

251

What is your name?	"Kedu áhà gi?" (keh-DO AH-HA gee)
Nice to meet you.	"Ọ een y." (AW DEE MM-MA)
How are you?	"Kedu kà ímèrè?" (keh-du kah E MEH-REH)
Fine, thank you.	"Ọ een y." (AW DEE MM-MA)
Welcome.	*Nnöö* (in-NOOR)
I can't speak Igbo [well].	"A nam a sú Igbo [ọfuma]." (AH nam AH sue EEG-BOW [AW-FOO-MAH])
Do you speak English?	"I na sú Bèké?" (EE na SOO BAY-KAY?)

Is there someone here who speaks English? "Ọ di onye nọ nga nweríkí súfù bèké?" (OR dee on-yeh NOR in-GAH weh-RI-KI SUH-foo beh-KEH)

I need your help. "Á chom kí nyém àkà." (AH chom een yeah-m AH-KAH)

Where is the toilet? "Ké ébé mpọsi dì?" (keh EH BEH mmPosee D)

FAMILY NAMES

Father   *Nnà, Mpá* (NN-nah, mm-PAH)

Mother   *Nne, Mmá* (NN-neh, mm-MAH)

Older Brother   *Nwannem Nwoke* (WAHN-NEM woah-kay)

Older Sister   *Nwannem Nwanyi* (WAHN-NEM WAHN-yee)

Younger Brother   *Nwannem Nwoke Ntà* (WAHN-NEM woah-kay NN-tah)

Younger Sister   *Nwannem Nwanyi Ntà* (WAHN-NEM WAHN-yee NN-tah)

Grandfather   *Nna Nna/Nne* (NN-nah NN-nah/NN-NEH)

Grandmother   *Nne Nne* (NN-NEH-NN-NEH)

Uncle   *Dédè* (DEH-deh)

Aunt   *Àntí* (ahn-TEE)

Husband   *Dí* (DEE)

Wife   *Nwunyè* (WEE-yeah)

Son   *Nwam Nwoke* (WAHM woah-kay)

Daughter	*Nwam Nwanyi* (WAHM WAHN-yee)
First Son	*Ókpárá* (OK-PAH-RAH)
First Daughter	*Àdá* (ah-DAH)
Last Child	*dụdụ nwa* (aw-DOO-DOO wah)
Grandchild:	*Nwa Nwa* (WAH-WAH)
In-law:	*Ọgọ* (aw-goh)

PHOTOS

"Ihedigbo Clan"

From the top: Emeka, Nathaniel(Nate), Apollos,
Onyinyechi (Onyii), David, James, and Rose.

Apollos in Umuawa , Abia State, Nigeria

Ihedigbo Family

Emeka, david, Nathaniel, James, Rose, Onyii

Ihedigbo Children

Nathaniel, David, Emeka, Baby James, Onyii

Ihedigb Family

Position:
Defensive Back

Height:
6'1"

Weight:
210 lbs

Birthdate:
12-3-83

College:
Massachusetts

Hometown:
Northhampton, MA

44

www.jamesihedigbo.com

James
IHEDIGBO

NEW YORK JETS 2007 to 2010

DR. ROSE IHEDIGBO

THE SUPER BOWL

As this book was going to print, Superbowl XLVII was played in New Orleans, Louisiana, on February 3, 2013. James Ihedigbo and the Baltimore Ravens faced the San Francisco Forty-Niners in a game notable for a furious comeback attempt by San Francisco after a 35-minute power outage in the Superdome. Ultimately, the Ravens held on for a 34-31 victory to become the 2012 World Champions.

Ingram Content Group UK Ltd.
Milton Keynes UK
UKHW020627210323
418905UK00014B/1073